What People Are Saying About This Book

Subtly we hand over our spiritual rights to the enemy of our souls, and as he tells us we have the right to remain silent, the hopelessness of doom chains our hearts to his darkness. Now, walk out of the caverns of darkness, take the keys of life in Christ, as you end *The Affair With Death*.

Apostle Winston Trought,
Covenant On The Rock Ministries International,
Cape Cod, MA

The Affair With Death opens your eyes to the forces of darkness waging war against you, and reveals the power and authority of God, available to those who want to win the war.

Rev. Richard Rego,
Trinity Methodist Church,
Martha's Vineyard

The Affair With Death

The Affair With Death

JACQUELINE TROUGHT

Clovercroft Publishing

The Affair With Death

© 2015 by Jacqueline Trought

All rights reserved. No part of this book may be reproduced or transmitted in any form or by any means, electronic or mechanical, including photocopying, recording or by any information storage and retrieval system, without permission in writing from the copyright owner.

Scriptures marked (NKJV) are taken from the New King James Version®. Copyright © 1982 by Thomas Nelson. Used by permission. All rights reserved.

Scriptures used by permission of *The New Jerusalem Bible*. New York; London: Doubleday; Darton, Longman & Todd, 1985.

Published by Carpenter's Son Publishing, Franklin, Tennessee.

Published in association with
Larry Carpenter of Christian Book Services, LLC.
www.christianbookservices.com

Cover Design by Mark Neubauer

Interior Design by Adept Content Solutions

Printed in the United States of America

978-1-942587-08-8

Dedicated to my husband Winston Trought, for his spiritual insight and great leadership ability that keeps propelling me forward; to my beloved Amaya, who teaches me the sweetness of love; to my son, Joune, who brings joy to my heart; and to my mother, Egna, who keeps me on my knees before a holy God.

Contents

	The Preface	xi
Chapter 1	The Assignment	1
Chapter 2	The Enchanter	9
Chapter 3	Valley of the Shadow of Death	19
Chapter 4	Ghetto Penthouse	31
Chapter 5	Desperate Me	39
Chapter 6	Puppet in the Pulpit	51
Chapter 7	Losing Ground	79
Chapter 8	The Last Drink	89
Chapter 9	Destroy the Evidence	97
Chapter 10	Shatter the Hold	113
Chapter 11	The Gig Is Up, Way Up	125
Chapter 12	The Violent Take It by Force	143
Book 2	A Book of Prayers	171

The Preface

We live in an age where the full measure and the pungency of evil is not done in secret. Perhaps less than a century ago, the work of detectives was highly necessary because the diabolical trails of evil were found, and the spectators were left in shock without proof. Nicodemus told Caiaphas the High Priest that the Jewish law did not sentence a man before it heard him, and even today laws everywhere bring men to the justice table of defense.

However, much is changing before our very eyes. Gun violence, the massacring of innocent children, beheadings, stranglings, and varying sorts of brutality are captured then displayed over and over so our hearts may become filled with the fear of evil and then become angry at Jehovah God, for not stepping in and curing the earth of sin.

People everywhere who have not bothered themselves with seeking the face of the Lord God Almighty are often the ones who question, *Where is God, and why did He allow this to happen.* Then those who know the love and faithfulness of our Sovereign

Lord are forced to provide an answer or defend our God trying to prove that God exists, that He did not really allow evil, while stumbling in our hearts as we see the gall of sin displayed horrifically daily all around us.

The reality is that when blame is to be passed, man will subtly deny truth and discard it as nonsense or figments of the mind in order to cast the judgment set in his determination. No one ever asked in the face of diabolic evil, *where is Satan and why did he allow this*? I have never heard anyone say, *this act is from the pits of hell and we will not stop until we have erased the face of darkness from the earth.*

Why are we so against the Almighty God? Why haven't we turned our anger onto Satan? Why don't we talk about the spirit world, why don't we look evil in the eye and call it evil, why do we mourn with agonizing confusion over death? Because we know deep in our hearts that the earth is greater than man, and even greater still, is the unknown of the spirit world which will eventually swallow us all.

However, to those who have been wise enough to tap into the wealth of that which boggles the mind of intellectuals and fools alike, being swallowed up by the God we serve becomes life everlasting and an eternity to enjoy the bliss of the God we trusted in the middle of the storm.

We have learned that the wages of sin is death. Therefore, we carefully guard our hearts against evil, and in simple faith humble ourselves to seek the face of the one true God. When sin knocks at our door, we reject the call, because we know that sin brings death, and where there is no sin, death cannot have its way. It is true, in order for death to toll its bell, we must give the monster permission, and as soon as the heart gives in, or says yes by partnering with evil, death grips its prey for eternity.

Let death not deceive you with enticing words or the fear of tomorrow, but rather lend your heart unto righteousness, and partner with truth, because to as many as believed on Him, to them He gave power to become the sons of God.

CHAPTER 1
The Assignment

She knew it was time to go into the parlor again. Every so often her mother would fidget around the house, nervously looking over her shoulder. She could count on dinner to taste like mush baked into stale bread soup. She could count on her father being away from dinner that night, and she could count on the nightmares she would have later.

The parlor was the most lavish room in the house. It was only used to entertain important friends. Marbled walls etched and contoured for beauty, with Roman chandeliers dimly lit to reflect a hue of peaceful colors, Venetian blinds surrounded by Victorian swags and pleats, and the walls decorated with ancestral portraits. Her mother walked over to the Tudor cabinet and retrieved the family heirloom quilt with its myriad designs. The cloth was old and soiled, with a sickeningly moldy smell, but her emotionally broken mother robed herself in the treasure, knelt and wept.

The mantle seemed to possess strange powers as her sobs ebbed into chants. Soon she would circle the room placing her right hand on the portraits and reciting their names. Charles Buckenshide of Toulouise, Mary Buckenshide of Toulouise, Janey Elsmire of Wendaroke; on and on it went. She had explained that the ancestral control of their towns left them with, not only inner powers, but also territorial dominance, which was now part of their names and their acknowledged power. They were still there; their souls kept watch, and she would draw from their powers in her darkest moments.

Just before the parlor session ended, her mother would fetch the glass jar on top of the Tudor and carefully arrange its contents in a circle on the prayer mat before them both. After her familiar chant she would prick the tip of her first finger on the right hand and press the blood into the quilt.

It did not take long for her to realize she had been gifted with strange powers. She remembered the day Eienster Shambly wanted to take the lizard-shaped pencil her mother had brought back from her trip to Italy. Her lips released the growl, "I dare you," and scared not only Eienster but also herself. She was excited about the thing and wished and begged that she could have it again. Many times she just pretended she had it, but soon it came back. At first she became the envy of her class, but weird activities began happening, and then she became the eyesore. She was the only girl in her class without any friends. Of course, several girls felt sorry for her and shared lunch with her on occasion, but that usually lasted only a day. Some gruesome unexplainable sound or action would end the session, and she would be alone again.

Angelique was different. Her heart-shaped lips and bewitching smile could quench the raging of a mad dog. Often Angelique was at her side, saying quiet words she just could not understand, but words that warmed her on the inside and made her feel like Heaven had come to Earth.

Sadly, Angelique's musical charm was not around for her crowning moment at the gymnasium locker room. On that day a few of the boys, led by Mockale Samson, decided to have a romp with her imaginary friend. As usual, she was the last one to use the locker room because it was the painless route from the insults and the taunting gossip of the other girls.

She was stuffing her gym shoes into her bag, but they fell to the floor. Mockale had grabbed the bag and emptied her books onto the floor. Stick-Boy Charlie grabbed her hair, pulling her to the back of the room. Fatso Brown ripped at her blouse and pushed her onto Charlie. The boys erupted into laughter.

"Show us the monster." Mockale could hardly get the words out between his laughter.

"Is he in your shorts?" Fatso's eyes were glaring with the glint of evil. "Let's strip her."

He rushed towards her while Stick-Boy Charlie yanked her towards him. Mockale grabbed at her hand but collided with Fatso because Stick-Boy had shoved her from the back. Each boy took his turn, pushing and shoving while grabbing and loosening her clothes.

Her heart bled with helpless cries of mercy: her lips stuttered with pleas of pity: and her head, spinning out of control, became lighter with each passing second. Fatso's laughter morphed into the bellow of a raging bull as he skidded his heel into the tile, pivoted, then wielded his knees into her gut, pounding her onto the wall. Shock melted her brain into numbness and when her head hit the mortar, everything went black.

Her mother's account was that each of the boys was taken to the hospital for treatment. Fatso had a broken arm, Stick-Boy Charlie's leg was sheered on the wall, and Mockdale's jawbone was broken in two places.

School held nothing for her; she dropped out a year before graduation. She had no friends and she learned nothing. Everyone knew her as *the girl with the friend*. Her mother and father were now divorced, and he did not acknowledge that she existed. Her mother was ill and frail, and they lived off the wealth of the estate.

To ease the boredom of her days, she would take long trips to the country, sometimes returning home days later. At other times she would sit and meditate, traveling miles in her meditation and doing things she dared not tell, perfecting the art of manipulating minds.

Her shop was in the center of the business district, and she exerted mental control over her territory. She lured people in and emptied their wallets with telepathic control. The heart of her readings were to capture the soul of each client and chain it beyond its will to function outside the realm of her supernatural wisdom. Hundreds were served up and marked for life. Her tongue was like the ink pen of destiny, she spoke and the future came alive. She attended to the lives of the affluent all the way through to the homeless. She had cured a homeless man with words of compassion, and now he owned the barber shop three doors away.

She had bonded with every demon in hell, but now he had the honor of coronating her, he was chosen to escort her to the throne of the one she served, to be reserved in chains for breaking the "Heart and Mind Code". The first rule is that the heart belongs exclusively to the master. It shall not be engaged to bring goodwill to mortals, and the mind must channel the knowledge of darkness to establish its powers over men. She had turned soft, exerting control to build her territory, not her master's.

It would change everything—rank, authority, territory. Many were outwitted, or would it be better to say, *disfigured* for this placement to be handed to him. It was hard work, in fact it was a miracle to conjure such guile; the secret was consistency, never break stride. Today would crown the countless patterns of managed misdirection, watching the senses twirl with ecstasy and the heart thump with a tune that rocks the mind into a frenzy. Certainly, for this coronation, a beat must be produced that will have the whole earth singing.

Compared to outwitting the others to gain this rank, the assignment was easy. There was not much in the way of persuasion left to accomplish. She was already a basket case. Great show, but each day claimed so much effort; and the pills, she never forgot the pills. They contained the life she needed. The only bright spot was seeing his face, and the sparks danced in her eyes. Every plan had been rehearsed—the time, the location, the emotions, and even the ring would be there for additional support. They had better be there, his support had advanced their rank. Not to worry, it was nine o'clock and he must be at his post.

Tick, tick, tick, his heart bounced to the rhythm of the clock. Just a gut feeling that it would not go as planned. It was a bleak day and the atmosphere was dense with a morbid sense of blackness. But that's how it is; the foul odor of his person oozed like a mist, announcing his presence, while dampening the senses of each passerby. He wished it could be controlled, but how else would he mark his turf?

Tick, tick, tick. The wait was unusual, upsettingly unusual. She has the discipline of angels.

"Urgluged." A gurgle erupted from his gut, and the foul smell of a million rotted gobies filled the air. Then he remembered that he had made himself visible. "Quick, a cigar." He felt around in his pockets. "Quick, mask the black air with smoke." Foul language flowed over and over. It was not just the fumbling for the non-existent cigar that produced his anxiety, but he remembered the phone call she got last night. Something was wrong; he knew it. Time! She was late. She was never late.

His rage was building, bubbling, overflowing. Someone must pay, anyone. "Slouggge, glub, glub!" the rage poured over the miserable homeless man near the gutter. The ring that controlled him was a group of amateurs, they always got it wrong. It did not matter that he messed up their plans. The homeless man began cursing as he felt rage pouring into him, the pain in his heart becoming unbearable. It felt like death.

He floated silkily through the air. He knew he was seen, but that was the least of his worries. He had used up so much of his powers at the thought that he was upstaged, did he now possess enough reserve to carry out the plan?

As he hovered over the house, he could see her writhing in pain. Great, even from a distance he controlled her. He may just have enough to finish the job. What is that?

"Flipping battle-sticks. Angels? Help!" The cry came from his lips, weak and muffled. They had him silenced. He circled. His odor was there, the pain could be heard miles upwards, but it was mixed with, mixed with? What is that? "Master," the shout ruptured the heavens, "someone is praying!"

CHAPTER 2

The Enchanter

It seemed like a beautiful day. The sun was just beginning its routine climb through the window close to the lattice. In a few minutes it would become fiercely bright and connect the delicate green and orange that stained the broken window to the left. Then the alarm would puncture the breathtaking picture with its miserably dreadful *gwaak*. He laid there rummaging through the day's activities, and drifting slowly back to dreamland.

Gwaak, gwaak, gwaak. It never failed to annoy him, but it never failed to get him moving. Like clockwork he rolled over, while checking his breath, and slapped the snooze button, then came the one-eighty turn to the woman who held all his dreams. Her wake-me-up-gently tones still delighted his senses. He pulled her to him but could feel that gentle resistance. He muttered a silent prayer, *not this morning, let today bring me luck.*

Perhaps his romp was too predictable, perhaps he had to develop a new style, perhaps his breath was the stay, perhaps, perhaps, perhaps. His body was flushed with mixed emotions, anger blended itself with desire, love grappled with despair, hope just hung on, to what? The romp got a little aggressive and her eyes flew open, and not admiringly. With a strong grasp she removed his arm, turned, and got out of bed.

"That's it!" He sighed, the kind of sigh that deflates everything. He looked around at his perfect castle, nothing meant anything anymore. Misery and fear and anger roamed around his head. He tried searching for answers, but they seemed to be the same answers he had supplied so many times, including the few times he escaped to those harmless pictures where the women indulged his uttermost fantasies. He did not want to face her. Rejection was as strong as it had ever been. He was going to be late for work; he would lie. Frustration comforted his heart, his body had reached fever pitch, and fevers have a way of destroying potent brain waves.

How about working late tonight? Again? That did not seem to work in his favor; she showed no interest. The shower interrupted his brain fog. His eyes crept into the shower and gloatingly expressed their appreciation.

Gwaak, gwaak, gwaak. Profanity escaped his lips. "Where did that come from?" He jumped up, dressed himself, and left without a word.

Can emotions really change a beautiful day? Thoughts reeled through his head miles per second. Let go of the perfect marriage and relax a little. Give yourself a chance to enjoy the creative expression within. Explore your options, that's life. Parking was horrible as usual. What's the point? He would park near the janitorial work station and walk.

Life had been so good—money, house, career, and a wife who was the envy of all. Perhaps she had found someone else. Silence were the only words she spoke lately. Always too tired or too busy to...

"Oh, oh, I'm so sorry." The softness of her body echoed in his bones and blended with soft angelic chirps of apologies. His heart began a dance, but his body froze as his eyes scanned the delicate frame opening up the fabric and entering in without permission. She extended her hand to polish off her apology. Her fingers were tiny, her skin was soft, she was an intense picture of painful beauty, a goddess of allure. His eyes drooled and his senses pointedly expressed a rush of hormones that made him second cousin to Pinocchio.

It was the end of the day, and he had looked at her business card over a hundred times. He was not the unfaithful type, he had been with one woman his entire life, and that's the way it would be. But this goddess with her sweet voice had mesmerized his philosophy. He had enjoyed the taste of her lips throughout the day, and any woman that apologized must be sent from God. Finally he made the call; the conversation lasted just under two hours.

It was three weeks later and they had talked almost every day. Her words were always kind and soothing. Tonight they would meet at Misty's on the farther side of town where the rivers met; he would be late going home, but it could be called a late night at the office. His wife was a bit more attentive this past week, his morning routine was now a ninety-degree roll to the alarm and then the bathroom. He made small talk where necessary but was in his car in a flash. After work she was home earlier than usual but spent her time on the upstairs deck after her hour-long visit to the pond. He had tried his romp a few mornings ago, but he lacked the fire to proceed. Someone else was on his mind.

He had kept alive every second of the moment their bodies collided, however, he promised himself not to indulge his senses. He would have dinner, listen to the juices of her voice, wrap his mind around the taste, and exercise self-control. But as he followed the sunset out of town, his body pulsated as if he was riding a horse.

It was early morning, just an hour before dawn. He stood looking at the river only visible by the light of the moon, which formed the shape of an arrow as it cast its light between the trees. He had released eight months of energy tonight. She had curled in his arms and wept softly with joy after the first session. He watched her curled lips move as she expressed her delight, and he arched slowly to meet them, wanting to feel the expression inside rather than being hypnotized by the angelic sound. Then, over and over and over again, the night was not long enough. Each session conquered new heights and released new sounds; they could not get close enough. The treasures of love they expressed inside each other explored depths, charted new paths to satisfaction; a total abandonment of the senses, a letting go to the waves of gratification and allowing its appeal to take them beyond into the realms where reality faded into the bliss of heaven. This was love, this was what he had been missing—love.

She was asleep. He turned to look at the woman who gave him manhood in one night. He would never be the same. She was a picture of beauty, a goddess at love, hair tossed across the pillow, frame curled beneath the covers...how could this be wrong? He was innocently driven to this moment. All he wanted was a wife he could cherish till death. Instead, she changed course and chose to reject him. Rejection drove him to awaken the wellspring of youthfulness that was untapped. Tonight he became a man, he ruled, he reigned, he conquered and staked his flag of freedom. That's right, there was no turning back: he must find a way to make her his own.

The nights only got better, impossible as it seemed, and now he lived for six o'clock. As he grabbed his coat, a voice startled his preoccupied adventure.

"Ben, you don't hang around anymore, is everything all right?"

Not now, this conversation could have taken place at lunch. "Certainly," the lie rolled off his tongue as he walked briskly to the door. "Kathy and I are working on personal details, and I want to focus on keeping our marriage strong." He nodded courteously as he exited, not inviting another question.

I should get her flowers; the thought zig-zagged across his mind. *What if she doesn't like them*, Kathy doesn't. Wow, he just realized their time was spent feeding their pent-up appetites of intimacy. What about her family, was she ever married, did she have children? He smiled, three months of sacred romance, no time for anything else. She made no requests, asked no questions, and was comfortable in his manhood; such trust. His mind reeled at the thought. Tonight he would ask; after all, soon she would be his wife. These past three months made him into a new man. He pulled into the right lane, and turned on the corner to Baron Street.

"What shall I find for you today?"

"I am searching for a gold necklace with a sapphire and diamond heart-shaped pendant."

"I have just what you are looking for."

It was stunning, a little overpriced, but it spoke the language of his heart.

Oh no, traffic flooded the highway, he would be late. He could hardly keep still; sitting in traffic was never so brutal. He held the box that bore his token. Tonight he would serenade her, share his heart, confess that he was married, but express the token of his sincerity to be free to enjoy her forever. He was sure she would feel the same. He could not wait to see those delicate lips form the words, *I love you.* He had not heard those magic words in years. Kathy was as cold as ice, and her language was even colder, but this was no time to think of Kathy, he just wanted this moment to be perfect.

He pulled into the motel and parked towards the back, just a few feet from his room. It had begun to feel like home. There was only one lady at the desk who made him uncomfortable. She was pleasant and courteous, professional even, but something about her motherly eyes haunted him. She would dismiss him with, "Give my regards to Mrs. Casse," with a tone suggesting she knew it wasn't Kathy.

He was dizzy with excitement. He wanted to hold her in his arms like a baby and look into those flickering eyes as she unfolded her life story. At the end he would cuddle her softly and place the symbol of love around her neck to hang over her heart, then he would tell her his story and together they would begin the journey into forever.

As he inserted the key into the door, an eerie feeling came over him, causing his body to almost slump to the floor. He collected himself, smiling at the thought that his ticker was beating too fast. The room was dark, the lights were off, the air was heavy, stuffy, almost to the point where breathing took an effort. Then there was that sound.

"Oh my God, she is in trouble," he muttered, as his heart pounded even harder. His eyes scanned the bed, the floor; no, she was in the bathroom.

He bounded across the room and swung the bathroom door open with forced strength. Somehow it felt like the building was on fire and the room was filling with smoke, even though it was not. The door bounced back, pushing him aside, but nothing prepared him for the sight.

Adia was kneeling on the floor, rocking back and forth, her eyes bulging, her face contorted, with lips pulled back exposing her teeth, gurgling then hissing like an angry snake. A doctor's bag with ropes and a steel knife lying on top was sitting in the wash basin. She did not see him; she was somewhere else. The tones from her throat sounded like the rage of an argument, a quarrel between two deadly rivals. The boiling sounds chilled his spine and his knees began to buckle; his palms were sweating, but the bones in them were icy cold.

Help her. Run. No, help her. I say *run*. The frenzy in his mind was heinous. He grasped the door for support as the dense invisible smog of the room began to suffocate him again, his feet felt stuck to the floor as if he was standing in a pot of glue.

The knife, the rope! Run, run!

He looked at her face again. It was not the face of the woman he had kissed and held so many times. Her body had begun to convulse as if something was inside moving from her head to her feet. As she throbbed on the floor, a syringe rolled from her body to his feet. He bent to pick it up, but instead he reached for the bag. A small vial inside was labeled Propofol 50 mg/mL.

His head swirled and his lips muttered his infamous swear "Jesus Christ." He fell backwards and onto the floor as if whatever had held onto him abruptly let him go. She raised her head and a gurgle erupted from her gut as if to silence his swear, yet she did not acknowledge he was there. Slowly she began to rise from the floor, not using her hands and feet but as if invisible hands aided her; she coiled, head to toe, then she was lowered to the floor again, and an unintelligible chant began.

"Jesus Christ, what is this?" She pitched sideways at the word, and a roll of duct tape and a red marker bound in the tape bounced from her clothes to the edge of the bath, then he noticed, the tub was filled with water.

Oh God, oh God! He didn't want to believe.

Run! The voice echoed in his body and seemed to give strength to his weakened limbs. He looked around: where was the door. Everything looked black. He knew where to find the door, but it was not there. A wall was in front of him, a black wall.

Run! Again the voice strengthened him. He did not want to look at her, it weakened his limbs and strangled his senses.

Just run, run! He did not have the strength to stand, so he began to crawl towards the direction of the door he had used so many times. He closed his eyes as he fumbled to the door—they were of no use, everything was black—but as he did the sounds from her gurgle began to pull him back from his escape. His thoughts became jumbled and he was not sure what he had set out to do. His icy cold body felt a burning rush of heat, like a cauldron of fire was lit inside his belly.

"Jesus Christ, this is hell," he muttered silently. The fire in his gut seemed to light the room and before him on the floor were his coat and the treasure he had brought in. He reached for them and instantly the room turned black. The gurgling chant, slow and soft, began its echo, pulling him backwards, moving his body to its sway. The sweet lips which had drunken his senses all these months penetrated his ears, and the gut-twisting gurgle began to sound like a cry for help.

His hands limply released his coat and his bag with the token to bind them together. Without thinking, he turned again toward the door as his body began to swirl with the desire to have her. His heart pounded with the love and memories of passion and joy that had tranquilized his world. How could I leave her when she needs me most? He pulled back the door to see the grotesque frame of her body levitated in mid-air the steel knife glistening in her hand and blood drooling from her gnarled lips. The sight knocked his senses into shock, rendering him helpless on the floor.

"Jesus, Jesus, help me, help me. Please God help me." The room lightened and he felt hands, invisible hands, scooping up his collapsed frame and hauling him to the door. Once outside, they dragged him to door of the motel's office and left him there.

CHAPTER 3

Valley of the Shadow of Death

"**E**at up, boy!" the next second my head was bashed into the bowl. Up, down, up and down again. The grip buried his knuckles and his ring deep into my scalp. The bowl escaped the third round by slipping to the side and off the rugged unfinished barks of wood nailed together as a dining table.

"Margo, get in here, the boy spilled his cereal." My mother came hurriedly into the room with a rag in her hands to clean up the mess.

"Woman, what's the tears for? Are you trying to make this boy into a wuss?" His backhand was swift as it connected with her jaw, and it returned as quickly to trap my efforts of escape, a smooth transition, developed by years of practice. My mother was on the floor, but she knew she would be helped mercilessly to her feet if she stayed down. She scrambled for the bowl and started toward the kitchen, but it was not over. "Woman, back here! Who is the man in this home?" This *dump*, he should have asked.

"You are, my dear."

"Now, grab that beam and teach this boy a lesson."

She tripped over her feet getting the piece of wood that held the window in place. I knew she did that on purpose. So many times she made a fool of herself to deflect the heat that was meant for me. His feet brought her back to an upright position, but not before it pummeled her to the wooden floor, all the while his hand skillfully wielding my frail body along. Thankfully I was not being dangled by the neck this time—my hair was long enough to be the perfect handle. He pulled her up to his chin as he thrust me to the side.

"You have not given me another son, and it's been six years. I know what you've been up to, but I want more boys. I need an army." His anger turned to a grin as he lowered her onto the table. Left, right, two more lefts. The blows brought blood gushing from her face. He slammed her body on the table and muttered, "Don't lose this one or you are dead."

Two days later my father was found dead at the back of the warehouse close to the train tracks. My mother bawled out her eyes for her friends and his parents, but as soon as they were gone she settled into a mode of satisfaction. Over the years she grew cold and distant. She lived like a ghost, spoke fewer and fewer words until she stopped speaking.

I had to grow up fast; put food on the table by whatever means I could. Most people thought I was too small to work, so they wouldn't hire me. I learned to steal to feed my mother.

"My son, life has its dark times, but you must keep the faith. Pray the Rosary seven times daily along with three Hail Mary's."

"Father, will that take care of the sickness I feel in my soul? It is like a brick weighing me down, and the nightmares get worse every night. I kill people in my dreams every night, and my father, who is always in these dreams, slugs and clobbers me if I hesitate; but when I wake up, it is so real. I remember the cold faces of the people I kill or I am in pain from the beatings; plus it feels like there are haunting spirits around that makes me want to lock away from everyone and just do evil."

"My son, God is with you. You must remember that at all times. *God is your shepherd, you lack nothing. In grassy meadows He lets you lie. By tranquil streams He leads you to restore your spirit. He guides you in paths of saving justice as befits His name. Even were you to walk in a ravine as dark as death you need fear no evil, for He is at your side. His staff and His crook are there to soothe you.* God is with you my son. I will see you at the next confession."

"Ha-ha-ha, good Catholic boy! You went to the priest, huh?" The deep rumble of mocking laughter echoed through his brain like the thundering of waters.

"Who are you, where are you?" There was a strong smell of suffocating sulfur. "Get away, get away from me." My eyes bulged with fear as I searched for my invisible enemy; my heart lunged and tightened with the force of a hammer, weakening my resolve to escape.

"How dare you talk to your father like that? Get up, you lazy bum, I have work for you to do. Sit around all day in a slump of pity. Get up!" Invisible hands and a compelling force bounced me against the wall. My body quivered in fright as I hit the edge of the table. Blood spewed from the puncture just below my rib. Quickly I scrambled to my feet and hurried to the door, moved by the force of the dreadful torment around me.

The hands of my father clawed at my back, pushing me forward. It was past midnight, I knew it: the street was empty. Squawking shrieks sounded from the sky above, then one by one, haunting ghouls swooped by me, roaring with the deafening mockery of shrieking laughter. My body was not my own, they controlled me. Their huge smelly bodies brushed against me, piercing me with unbearable pain. Their shrieks seemed to be a call for others to join in on the sacrifice, and I was their puppet, dragging my frail and limp body along to the agonizing demise ahead.

Some kind of ruckus was going on in the darkness a few feet in front of us. As we neared, I saw a woman stumbling around in circles with her hands covering her ears from the torment of the huge black monsters around her. Talk about monsters—the beasts were overpoweringly massive. One with a huge sickle in his hand barked a few orders, and they quieted for a chat. The uproar must have quieted for the woman as well because she leaned on a nearby tree then slid lifelessly down its bark to curl over into a ball, still covering her ears. The monstrous beast who possessed the sickle managed them all and kept the order for this mandatory meeting, where each beast listened quietly as he addressed them. Where did he come from? I had never seen his likes in my dream before.

I know I should escape; they weren't paying attention. I wanted to grab the girl and run, but my body was numb, almost trapped in its position. I didn't see my father even though I could see all of them, but he wasn't there. Perhaps he wasn't important to them and was dismissed; perhaps he was the wimp I always thought he was.

A quarrel was brewing as noise between them began, and I could feel the pains of the noise aching in my body. I could tell the girl felt it too; I could see her squirming. I turned to leave—it was a slow deliberate turn. I wanted to; I had to. I had had enough of this; if only I had a little help. The girl let out a whelp of a cry, and all eyes turned in question. I turned too, and blazes of angry fire swooped toward me. The first was my father. He lunged at me with his claws, claws I never saw before. His body was different also, just a head with a thin wispy frame that tapered off into a tail of black soot. The claws jabbed into my flesh with a distinctive message—defiance has a penalty.

The pain in my body was beyond agony, but nothing compared to the diabolically sickening penalty inflicted on the girl. Before my very eyes, a monster was assaulting her. My head spun and my bones no longer supported my body. The monster's eyes penetrated my soul, and I could feel him sucking from me the life he needed while thrashing the girl like a rag doll. Her clothes were gone now, and I knew what was coming next. It was an act of malicious brutality, nothing gentle or pleasing; she was the answer to a job that must be carried out to satisfy the curse that had been placed on her.

The mob was in a frenzy, a gleeful frenzy. Their cheers seemed to encourage the monster to intensify his brutality to her and drain more life from me. I watched in a daze, utterly weakened and powerless to help. When the monster had satisfied himself with the girl, my weakened body was laid in a pile on the ground. Shouts of freaky praises rang out from the ring, and then, like a rehearsed operation, they unrobed me savagely, taking my soul, taking what I can only explain as *me*, stripping my inner being. When each of the beasts became satisfied with his portion of my core, it was handed to the monster with the sickle, and when he had collected all, with a wicked grin, he disappeared.

I woke up. That was a wicked dream, and it was so real. I lay there replaying the agony of that poor girl over and over again in my head.

Boom, boom, boom. The knock on the door was loud, persistent, demanding.

"Manny, open up!"

It was Luas. I could scarcely turn the lock when he forced the door forward into my face, knocking me aside. He made no apologies. Luas was a true friend, my only friend. He lived across the hall and provided me with joints, booze, and most of my food. Life was beyond unpleasant. All my efforts to live normally were botched, everything except Luas.

"Manny, a woman was found half dead near the black creek. Someone beat the pulp out of her and raped her too." He paused for a second. "Manny, you look sick, what's up? Man, you got blood on you, all over you!"

"Went to get some food last night and got mugged. Got any soup or the ball? I feel like hell."

Luas unburdened himself of his fried rice, three different packages to make the ball, and two different bottles of overproof to make the soup. He continued to ramble about the half-dead girl and how everyone was making a big deal about it, but I blocked the words from my ears. I was getting weaker by the second, but I had to make the ball. I could barely combine the powders; my nerves were raw and my trembling hands showed it.

"Steady, don't waste the stuff." Luas began to help, looking into my eyes with pity, trying to calm my desperation for relief.

I did not want to wake up from this one, it was better to die than live for my dead father who controlled me. I could not wait for the syringe, Luas reached over to grab them but I was snorting already. Half way down the line, I reached across the table for the bottle of rum while still snorting along the trail. It fell. I dived after it with the strength of a drowning man, taking care not to spill the unmade cocktail. It was my hope; I needed to end it all. I raised my head with care to open the bottle and lost my balance but clutched the bottle. I landed on my side, opened it up, and drank for dear life. The room began to get dark. I could hear Luas screaming for me to stop. Darker, darker, red-black.

Across from me sat the kindest looking diabolical monster I had ever seen. He was so ugly it pained my eyes to focus on him. His voice so contrasted his features, I raised my eyes to listen.

"I need you, Manny. You have served me so well, I could almost say you are irreplaceable. A soldier of soldiers, every bid, every command precisely executed.

Surely you are not ready to retire; you are not ready to give up on me? Come with me."

He turned and I followed without moving my body. He walked down a dark hall, and about every ten feet or so we passed what seemed like corridors. I could tell strange things were happening inside. The first corridor was hot like a furnace and produced a fire that seemed to make the corridor itself. The screams from it were bloodcurdling and it smelled like roasting flesh. The second corridor was made of bars, strong huge bars connecting to each other to form what looked like gates. The beasts inside were busy receiving, disseminating, and executing instructions. Their language was unintelligible, but somehow I could understand a fraction of it.

The black-red monster turned into the third corridor, which had a lot of ailing people on the floors. Each person had a blackish-reddish beast around them. The beasts seemed to share their energy with the ailing, strengthening and encouraging them to get them back on their feet. The corridor was loud with mutters, not gentle, but more of a soft anxious, persuasive mutter spouting from the beast enabling ailing and unresponsive wills to desire life. My body gained strength as I moved by.

The creature that led me magnetically by his words and my will, walked through a door that creaked open for me. It was solid black inside. I could smell a dank stench: something had rotted; something had died. But the voices in this room were even more persuasive than those at the entrance of the hall. They sounded like prayers, desperate prayers for life. I got the sense that the monsters owned the people, and if they died, the monster's assignments on Earth were doomed, so they needed these bodies to stay alive to be used again and again. While moving along, I constantly bumped up against wet and clammy lumps of gel-hard clay. Soon, my eyes started to focus, and I saw what looked like trees: a narrow valley with huge trees lining its outskirts. The valley was piling over with mangled bodies, some on top of each other. Some were dead, others dying, others were being coaxed back to life.

Trees! Those were not trees. They were monstrous creatures that hovered in the air, bent over with talons spreading from many arms that clustered and formed arches. To support their position, they drew strength from the very faint. A murderous prayerful lament and wail poured from their limbs in a slimy drool that brought help to the valley. The strange slimy power was mingled with a foul smell and as I walked deeper into the abyss, I knew I was swallowing it all.

The black-red monster seemed to have reached his destination and turned to face me. There were no words, but I knew I should sit by the feet of this creature that was selected for me. I obeyed and wedged myself between two bodies. The black-red thing leaned over to my eyes, and I knew what to do.

I reached over to the body on my left and embraced it with a soft cuddle. The moans were familiar, I had heard the voice before, somewhere. The creature seemed pleased, and placed its hands on our heads. No words again, but it began to drool with a language I understood but did not know. Who were the prayers going to?

I settled into the embrace, as I did not know what else to do. I had given my will over to this creature, and like so many times before, they had work for me to do, work that they could not perform without me. Here I was in this no-outlet dungeon, half dead, willing to die, yet once again submitting my will to be used against my wishes. I was not sure what part of me did not desire to obey this beast. I did not want to belong to it, I did not want to obey it, I did not want to follow its lead, but I did—without any hesitation. I was its property, that was clear. Releasing the hold was a mystery.

I had trained my senses to become numb to pain and noise and unwanted intrusion, so I began to engage them to drown out these surroundings. I hugged the body closer. It felt warm and familiar. I knew this body, I had touched it before, I had enjoyed it before, I had shared this body with mine, I was dreaming, I was foaming, I was sick—it was the girl from last night.

The creature grabbed me by the gut and ripped at my heart, pulling it out through my stomach, just below my rib. I could tell it wanted to exchange my heart for his, so I could do nothing but carry out its plans fluidly. My heart would not let me. It got stuck, tied between my windpipe and caught on the edge of my last two ribs. Profanity rained like hailstones from the beast, but the creature above him disapproved and with one vicious swoop, he was sliced and blown away. I fell beside the girl, but this time my heart felt her pain, and the desire to help overwhelmed me.

"I am sorry," I whispered. "Can I make it right? Can I give you my strength?" She seemed to understand all that was going on. She leaned her head against my chest, and her body began to build warmth. I did not know what else to say or do. I wanted to take her out of the valley, but I was clueless where to start. I closed my eyes, searching for answers. I wanted God for her, to make her right, to give her life. How could I find Him? This felt like the valley of the shadow of death. Would He come down to hell and save us? Suddenly, I heard the words of the priest, "God is always with you, my son, God is always with you!"

CHAPTER 4

Ghetto Penthouse

"We find the defendant guilty, on six counts of murder." The monotone was low, almost laced with a tone of sadness, as if he knew. The verdict followed without the judge lifting his eyes from the table. The courtroom was silent for what seemed like forever—no one moved. Then suddenly, a shriek went off in his head. A madly deafening sound, wild and vicious, thundering, jarring his brain waves. The twitching and the trembling began, then laughter—mocking, taunting laughter.

Clack, clack. "Please stand."

The hands holding the cuffs were tattooed with the contorted face of the most hideous snake he had ever seen. He looked away, but the pattern on the floor reflected the face, now riddled with bullets, torn and ugly. He closed his eyes, trying to replace the ugly sounds with the rapid beat of his heart, but instead he heard a gurgling in his gut, erupting, getting louder. It was bubbling, coming up his throat; the steaming volcano was fuming through his nostrils. The guard backed off at the stench of the foul odor, allowing the hand-cuff to dangle from his left arm. Two other guards rushed in to help, but got just close enough when their speed was slowed to a robotic stride, then to a slow retreat. The sounds of murmuring from the few in the room got louder as they made a cautious rush to exit the room. The judge swung around in his chair, choosing safety instead of waiting on his majestic indulgence, *All rise*. The guard collected himself and mechanically slapped on the cuffs, sat him down, and headed out the back door.

It was two months that he had been wearing his four-piece suit in the penthouse. The stench of the cell was now a part of him. The guards did not come up to his cell; no one wanted to come near him. He had not eaten a meal in so long, he could not count the days.

Loneliness was a beast. It tortured his mind and built up such a strong desire to just hear a voice, a longing to see a face, to look into someone's eyes; his desire for touch was more than his desire for food, yet at the sound of life, the sleeping monster inside would rise up and choke his heart. His body would begin to burn, his head would twitch and roll, his eyes would poke out of their sockets, and his heart would swell with the strength of ten lions; rage would well up in him and his throat would bellow out the profanities of hell, while deep inside, a baby with outstretched arms cried, *save me, please save me.*

He always looked back to that fateful night, the night he gave his virginity and pledged forever, the night the ghoul clawed its way under his skin; the night that changed his life forever. Tears were in her eyes as he pledged his soul.

"You are mine forever: here is my heart, take it forever."

His kisses merged their minds bonding their souls, melting, becoming one, swearing never again to be separate. The night swept them away, their bodies melded, discovering and savoring all the sweetness of the tastes hidden beyond dreams. Her tears flowed and her sobs got louder. "I have never been loved, I have never been loved. Love me please, I need to be loved. Hold me, take me forever."

"Forever, this will never end, I promise you forever."

The wailing of her soul pierced his heart. He kissed her face, drinking her tears, nuzzling and rubbing his lips onto the water-drenched softness. Her arms encircled his masculine frame, pulling and pushing with the strength of her passion, then clawing and tearing, digging so deep, it hurt. He flinched, his head twitched and rolled with pain, but he shook it off. He could not stop now; he had found love, and pain was part of the package. The fury of her desire was riveting into his flesh, yet she seemed unconscious of the terror he began to feel.

Focus, focus, enjoy these feelings of pain, revel in the wealth of this love, don't turn back now! He turned off the pain and ignored the blood he knew was now flowing from her claws and began to reciprocate the desire to be one. Time lost its balance and failed to keep its rhythm while the heartbeats of frenzy took over and pulsated throughout the night. Bodies, clawed, sweaty, bleeding, energized beyond the potential of calories and passion, pushed past daylight without missing a beat. Hours later he awakened to bloody sheets, his body burning from the claws of the love he had found, and an empty bed.

He had managed to check the ghoul for the first three years in the pen. It only showed up in his sleep at night. But lately it kept taunting him again, crying for blood.

"Huh, huh, aggh."

Startled, he raised his head, searching the concrete walls and the air around him for the monster who kept him company. "Who are you, where are you?"

His heart ached. This mocking laughter had been his friend for years, it was the familiar sound of the time of offering and he knew what would follow. If only he could see the monster, he would destroy it and be free forever.

Brake fluid had done nothing to suppress the beast, in fact it seemed to trap the ghoul inside with spiky nails of an unseen hand clawing and twisting his organs until they bled. Four hours after taking them, he was on the john, passing blood. Bug juice did the same, but it sent him on a ride, juicing his brain and pumping his adrenaline, setting him on a hulk-like high that made him tear iron bars with his bare hands.

He did not sleep last night; as quickly as his eyelids drooped, it clawed into his chest. He would scream, awaken everyone, and have the entire block wracking. This morning he was a bag of misery, not to mention the flak from every lip down the hall.

A twist of fate: footsteps were coming, closer, closer. The baton rattled on the bars, coming closer. He felt good, really good. The demon must have been sleeping, his insides were quiet.

There were three of them. One held the door with his tool handy, the other un-keyed the chains from his hands and feet, and the other kept spitting on the floor. No one said a word as they watched his every move.

On the grounds, he sat alone. His insides were quiet, a true moment of peace. The ghoul had been restless, nervous; three years, no service, no honor, no blood. But why didn't it go somewhere else, choose someone else? He closed his eyes, closed out the noise around and settled...

"Hey Buck, you jacked or sopmen?"

His body flew three feet in the air. He hit the ground in a rage, spun on his feet, sprung for the crossbar, twisted it free from its welded joint, and flattened the victim chosen for the sacrifice, all in just under one minute.

A good fight was a stimulant to all in peels to vent anger and flex muscles, but the ground was empty in under two. A swarm of guards with guns and bats skated unto the field and pounded him onto the ground. As he was being pummeled and chained, he saw the poor fellow his ghoul had chosen, gasping for breath and convulsing .

"Mr. Stark, you have been asleep for over five days." Tiny gloved hands rested lightly on the shiny rails. "Seems like you needed that rest." Her eyes danced as she spoke. Her hair glistened with shades of bronze in the bright lights. He had never seen an angel before. He scanned the room slowly. Three uniformed men padded with weapons, feet spread firmly on the ground, were posted around the room.

The soothing voice continued. "You will find tubes in your arms, Mr. Stark. They contain all the necessary fluids you need to get you back on your feet in no time. I must also explain that you have been restrained, but our staff will be more than happy to get you anything you desire. Do you have any questions for me?"

His curious eyes, dazzled by the bright lights, were the first half, but adding to the query were his mutterings which asked so many more questions though they did not make sense to him.

"Sir, I can hardly hear you."

The gentle voice flooded his mind with peace. Her voice, her face! Where was he; who is she? She seemed to soothe years of anxiety in him. He shifted his body; it felt weak and almost lifeless. The ghoul, where was he? Her eyes, they carried beams of healing to his soul. She just stood there smiling, as if she knew what she was doing.

Slowly, she reached for her stethoscope, connected it to her ears, then began to touch him. Gentle healing poured through her hands. She reached over his heart, passing her love across his chest, her smile infusing its glow into his eyes.

"Rest, Mr. Stark, you are doing just fine. I will leave you to rest."

Her magnetism seemed to place the guards at ease. He took advantage of her advise and drifted back to sleep.

Time passed slowly. Others came and administered medical care, but he looked forward to her visits. At each visit, she explained more. He had suffered a few broken bones at the prison, been in an unconscious state for a few days, and now he was diagnosed with bacterial pneumonia and had to be placed under extreme care. His body was severely malnourished, and the feeding tubes were set up because, when they brought him in, he was unresponsive.

The hospital room felt safe, like a hide-away just for him. The ghoul had not been there, and its torment had completely ceased. He felt normal, safe, comfortable, desiring life, real life. He could remember his mother sitting across from him while they had hot cereal together. Her laughter was delightful. He could remember her chasing him around the house just for tickles. Then it was his turn to chase and tickle her. When he caught up with her she would hoist him in the air and spin him around, throw him onto the bed, and the chasing would start again. He remembered when Aunt Hatley came to get him. He remembered the cold evening at his mother's funeral. Life was never the same. He lost hope, he lost life, and he began desperately to wish for death.

It was not long before he was on his own. He carried a duffle bag with all he owned and drifted from town to town. He was often scorned and stiffed. He woke up every day with the aimless bitterness of nothing to look forward to, and death on his mind. Scuffle, beg, steal, or exchange food for a day's hire was typical. Many days, he would lay in a gutter and sip its water to quench his thirst or wet his sun-drenched face, then find his bed between stacks of hay; that was the path he traveled.

Then there was that lady, Mrs. Dlob, who took him in to help on the farm. She was just like his mother, and he cherished her. Caring for the farm was the least he could do. He made sure there was an increase in the produce each year, and the horses never looked so good. He learned to service the tractors and equipment, up before dawn and in by supper. She paid him wages, but nothing compared to the food. He ate like a horse, but she did not mind because she loved him. His heart bounded with joy, three years and counting.

Then there was Pickles, and Lilah, and soon he was on the run, hiding from his own shadow. She took his soul, his virtuous soul, and he never saw her again. Yep, she disappeared into thin air, even though he kept going back to Pickles hoping to see her. He craved no desire for another woman. Well, not really! But after Lilah, all the other women invoked a strange fire within him, a fire to mutilate and kill. That first girl, her face so battered, her eyes so troubled, her body twitching constantly; she was the first. She had a pull on him that scared him stiff. He still cannot recall the details of how she stopped breathing. She must have had a heart attack. In his fright he carried the poor thing up into the mountains and sat over her for days, mourning her loss.

Then it seemed like the lust of the beast increased. Its ugly laughter was the sign, and surely after, came another victim. Now his heart was sore, the hapless fellow on the grounds was perhaps the next to go, or was it his time? He had tried to take his life so many times since Lilah left the beast with him. Overdosing just made him stronger. How, when, where? He did not want to go back to the cell; he did not want to feel the beast again. He had to die.

CHAPTER 5
Desperate Me

It was that time of the night when her mother turned into a crone, a drink in one hand, a cigarette in the other, and the floor boards creaking from her constant pacing. Her words were low and bitter.

"Christie, get to your room, go!" Her mother followed behind her. In seconds, the door parted their company, and she heard the turn of the key and the footsteps dancing away into the distance. Each step bounced with the waves of her heartbeat until, *bang*, the hall door closed and there was silence. The full weight of the sadness filled her chest and flowed through her eyes. Tonight she would not fight it, she would not believe, she would not care. Tonight she would give in. Let the desperation crawl into her soul and feed at her heart, let fear cause her body to tremble with rage until her feet were wet from her bodily fluids. Her mother had rejected her again; now she would embrace it until she turned to stone.

She walked over to the closet, "You, come to me. Now!" She did not pause. "Child, you have no respect."

She turned and grabbed her hair brush then hurled it at the Monster doll. It hit the doll in the face, and the lifeless frame fell over. She walked over to the toy and clutched it by the legs.

"You ungrateful child, all I have done for you, and still you walk around this place with that ugly face full of misery. When are you going to appreciate me for being a good mother? You ought to be glad I love you, you ought to be so glad. My mother never loved me; she was mean and brutal. It was so bad in our house, once she got into a fit and I landed in the fireplace. Now sit still so I can brush your hair."

She began rocking back and forth as she held the doll tightly between her knees, stroking its hair furiously. "You evil thing, someday you are going to thank me for being a good mother."

"Thank you, mother." The hoarse croaking voice was low but audible. Her body stiffened, every organ within her chest formed into a ball and tightened to the point of bursting. Her hands froze, halting the fury of the strokes in mid-air. The clasp of her knees widened on their own accord as the tiny doll on whom she had spouted her meanest words began to swell. A nauseating smell began to fill the room as the tiny hands curled and gnarled, extending like a branch of dead wood with spiny limbs. The thing turned on its feet, black and feathery like a crow, feet that did not exist just a few seconds ago. The pointy ears had the most hideous eyes inside of them, and the cheeks were now puckered in a puddle of battered blood; instead of eyes, the thing had hideous dark holes and the lips were inverted, protruding out of the nose.

The bloody scream could be heard around the block. She ran blindly to the door, throwing herself against it trying to break its resistance, wildly rattling the knob. "Mom, Mom, please, please, no please." The bleeding cry for help was morbid. The door opened and her mother grabbed her.

"What, what is it?" Her mother was as frightened as she was. She could not respond. Shaking with sobs of fright and relief she buried herself between her mother's legs and pushed her out of the room. The questions kept coming, and the continuous answers were the frightened sobs of the quivering body. Her face was swollen, as if poisoned, and her body hot with fever. Her mother's voice began to quiver. She led the child into the living room, where her male friend relaxed on the couch with a glass of whiskey in his hand and a pleased grin on his face. Her mother sat down by the dining table and held her daughter's face in her hands, she needed to take a good look.

"Christie, tell me what happened!" But her daughter had already passed-out.

It was three days later and she had just begun to regain her strength. The garbage man was now hoisting the bin into his truck. He would dart across the street for the Miller's trash, then away with that thing. She had managed to wrap it in an old *binkie*, then stuff it in a bag, carefully watching each moment to see if it knew where it was going. She unearthed the kitchen garbage, her hands smeared with rotted foods as she buried the doll at the bottom of the bag. She stuffed the trash over the package and sat down to watch her mother carry it off to the bin outside. Her sigh was deep and long as the truck geared up and rolled off to collect more garbage.

Her mother had not worked at the mill for months. She complained about the long hours and the few dollars it offered. She complained about how expensive food had become and kept wishing for the right job to come along so she could afford everything. It would have been a treat to have something else except bread and milk or beans and sausage.

Frequently, her mother took her to the doctor. On these trips her mother always wore a new dress and spent hours fixing her hair and makeup. At the doctor's office, Christie had to sit quietly in the waiting room while her mother got her regular checkup. The next day, her mother was on the phone to the school, reporting that she had another letter from the doctor saying her daughter was ill and had to stay out of school for a week.

Next came the frenzy of packing and complaining. "You move way too slow. Did you get my red shoes; you know I need them? Where are the pain pills? Go get them! I wish your grandmother would take you; you are just a handful." On and on, endlessly, until she paused for her drink.

They left the house at about five o'clock and drove into town, then found their regular parking at the back of Raff-Taff. It would be her home for the next few days, with her own room and her own window. The door was locked on the outside, and usually, someone brought food, at least once per day. Her mother came in just before dark each day to look her over. Sometimes she looked tired; other times she was drunk. When she was drunk, she was most kind; once she held her daughter in her arms and cried, then looked into her eyes and spoke a million apologies without moving her lips.

Next week would be school again, but it was almost impossible to follow the excessive talking of the teacher or keep up with the mountain of things to write. She wished for a place to hide, a room for herself with a window, just like the one at Raff-Taff where she could see almost the whole city. Everyone talked so much, smiling and sharing stories; it was too much. She looked forward to first-bell, when no one could wait to go to the playground, and she could hide away in the classroom and watch the parking lot from the window. Mrs. Shale had given up pleading with her to go make friends and have fun. These days she brought her fruits and sweet treats for her moments of silence.

It was the weekend and her mother was on her ranting high again. She had been cleaning all day but nothing was clean enough. She paused to curl her hair and put her make-up on, but started cleaning all over again.

The knock on the door frightened her, as if it were a death sentence. She circled the room twice, touching her hair and straightening her dress, before finally opening the door. It was Mr. Curvil. This was his first time back since the Monster doll night-of-horror.

Her mother opened the door slightly, then started blabbering and stuttering, not making much sense. He placed his hand on the door, opening it wide to let himself in. He pressed his body against hers as his hand reached around her waist. He leaned and whispered into her ear while his eyes scanned the room. His eyes found Christie in the corner near the liquor stand and his lips widened into a crooked smile. At the end of his ear-nibbling assurance, her mother released a sigh which sounded more like a groan.

He reached into his pocket and handed her an envelope. "Take care of yourself and the little princess for me. I will be out of town for a month. I will see you when I get back." He pressed his face into her cheeks, smiled, and left.

Her mother closed the door, and leaned on it in silence. Her face was white, but her eyes glinted with joy. The agitation was still in her feet as she ambled to the couch. She was about to recline her head when the envelope fell from her hands. She reached over to pick up the package but gasped at the stack of hundred dollar notes which had fallen to the floor. She raised her head, her jaws glued apart as her head turned towards the door—there was silence. She retrieved the treasure and dumped it in her lap. Christie walked over to the couch to sit beside her and muse in the shock of her mother's excellent luck. It was a tender moment as her mother stroked her hair, dazed at her good fortune.

"We don't have to go to Raff-Taff for weeks." A restless silence settled over her mother as she drank her way into the night. Guilty surrender mingled with prancing fear plagued her mind, but it was clear, long before the night was over, that her mother was bought.

They pulled onto the car lot, and her mother's eyes glistened with glee. She pasted her forehead against the window, thinking how lovely it would be to have one of these shiny new cars. A tall gentleman, with glasses tipped on his nose and an awkward stride that sent his feet in opposite directions from each other as he walked, came hopping over and enthusiastically introduced himself.

"It is a fine morning and anything I can do to make this a better day will be my pleasure."

Her mother glided out of the car, slithering her body against the car as she got the door for her daughter. "It is a fine morning indeed and I believe you will be just the person I need to make my day."

"My name is Samuel, and I am one of the managers here on staff. Let me guess, you are about to treat yourself to something special."

Her mother's smile was inviting. "Mr. Samuel, you have a way with words."

Her mother turned to her, "Get in the car!"

She knew what to do. From the car she watched as her mother's body excitedly animated itself, complementing her soft brilliant smile and her flickering eyelashes. Her mother strolled over to a sporty red model, sat on the hood, and continued her speech. The salesman did not seem to say much, but after a while, bowed himself from the waist and gestured his hand towards Christie. He walked to the car and opened the door.

"Little Miss Christie, we have a little treat for you, come with us." He took her hand and helped her out of the car. Once inside, he walked to a desk and pulled back the chairs.

"Well, are you sure we can have the best price possible?" Her mother's tone was soft and pleasurable.

"Absolutely. In fact, I am reducing the cost and offering the car at the manager's special, and I am doing it because of this little angel you brought with you today."

Her mother sat down. Disappointment plagued her face for a fleeting second, simmered to register misunderstanding, then settled into, *I got what I wanted.*

The salesman took his seat and ruffled through several stacks of papers. Back and forth he went, but it wasn't long before the deal was complete.

"Miss Christie, before you go, let me make good on my word. You are the preettiest little five-year-old I have laid eyes on in a long time, and I want to let you know that you have a heavenly Father who loves and cares for you. Now, He wants you to know that you can talk to Him anytime you wish. If things are going well, just believe in your heart He is by your side and thank Him. When things are not going well, do the same, and ask Him to make those bad things stop or go away, and He will. The only thing He asks in return is that you love Him and be a good child. Don't be mean, or ugly, or disobedient. If you can promise Him to be kind and gentle and obedient, He will promise to always protect you. Can you do that for your heavenly Father, Miss Christie?"

She smiled, "Yes sir, I will."

Her mother took her hand to lead her away.

"Let me invite you to church, Mrs. Crater."

"Oh, that is so kind of you."

"In our church you and little Christie will find a lot of help and good friends. You should come and see."

Her mother's body began its own rhythmic movement to tunes that no one else could hear. Her bashful smile combined itself with a frown that asked, how far should I go, or is this fatherly advice?

"Congratulations on your new car, I know you both will enjoy it."

It must have been the feel of the new car, but something made her more excited than she had ever been. No one had ever been so kind to her as that car man. She could not even remember all he said; she just knew she had met the kindest person in the whole wide world.

Her mother dropped her off and picked her up from school every day. Mrs. Shale and the children were friendlier, and the classwork made more sense. They had not gone back to Raff-Taff or the doctor in a long time. Mr. Curvil was invited to join them for dinner, and his visits became more frequent. Sometimes he helped with her homework, and somehow, it made her mother very happy. He was not there on weekends, so her mother made trips into town to shop.

The nights Mr. Curvil visited, she knew bedtime followed immediately after dinner, and she did not wait to be told. Recently it seemed Mr. Curvil was there early in the mornings to have breakfast and began offering to take her to school. After a few mornings of declining, her mother finally said yes.

Riding with him to school was strange. His driving was not steady, and he was not as friendly as when he was in the apartment; his conversation was limited to cursing under his breath at passing drivers for their inconsiderate driving. She choked back her undigested breakfast that made several attempts to decorate his black leather seats; she held her head back and counted the lights lining the streets, desperately waiting to see the white brick building of her school.

"I will pick you up this evening, Christie, your mother signed me on to help her get you from school."

His happy tone frightened her, turning her face white. She could not decide what was so discomforting about the ride with Mr. Curvil. It was different riding in her mother's new car since the day the car man talked with her. What did he say? Something about being protected, if I was kind... I had a Father somewhere that would help me if anything went wrong. Okay, I will be really kind today.

Fear stayed with her all day. Mrs. Shale noticed and came over to the window at first-bell. "I brought your favorite today." She held out her hand with the chocolate-covered peanuts.

Christie smiled and reached out to accept them.

Mrs Shale held onto her tiny hands. "Christie, do you know your heavenly Father loves you and watches out for you every day?"

"Why does He watch?" The question was a tough one to answer.

"Well, He loves you so much, He never wants to leave, so He just goes with you everywhere and watches out for you."

"How do you know my father? I've never met him!"

"Okay, every person has two fathers; one who lives on Earth and another who lives in Heaven, whom we call God. God can see everything that happens in our lives, so He sends His angels to protect us, especially when we ask."

Mrs. Shale patted her hands as she let them go. Christie knew that the other children at school had fathers, they were men who came to pick them up. Did Mrs. Shale and the car man meet her father? She did not want to ask.

In his car, Christie counted the light posts back to the house. Neither of them spoke. At dinner her mother was giggly and excited, talking about being a family and spending more time together, but Mr. Curvil was more enthusiastic about her great cooking.

Again, Mr. Curvil was at the house bright and early for breakfast, but after breakfast, he went into her mother's room to dress for work. Today he did not wear his usual shirt and tie, he just wore slacks. As she settled in the backseat of the car, he reached over and handed her a huge box, beautifully wrapped, and her name written on it in bold red.

"I have been shopping for you Christie, go ahead, open it."

He pulled out of the driveway as she began to tear away at the shiny paper. Inside were different sized packages wrapped in colorful paper. She opened the first gift and exclaimed in disbelief, "Ooh, these are nice, my friend at school has one of these slippers."

"Go ahead, there is more."

She could not believe how many things there were. She tore away at each wrapper with joy. She did not notice the litter as the toys and shoes and trinkets piled up around her. She held up her head, eager to take a few to show her friend at school—the kind girl in her class. School, where was this? Where were the lights, the shops?

"Where are we? Can I show some of these to my friend at school today?"

"Today we are not going to school. I have a friend I'd like you to meet. He lives outside of town. Your mother said I could take you to meet him."

"Okay." She paused to digest his words. "Can we take my Mom too? I bet she would like to meet your friend too."

"She wanted to rest today. Tomorrow she has a lot planned." His voice was reassuring, but he did not turn to look at her.

"Mr. Curvil, are you my father?"

"Your father? Why would you ask that?"

"Well, yesterday my teacher told me that I had a father somewhere, and he would protect me if anything ever went wrong. Are you my father?"

The car swerved to the other side of the road. He wrenched at the steering trying to direct the vehicle out of danger, but it would not budge. Frightful swears poured from his lips and his hands shook forcibly as if someone invisible was fighting the steering from his grasp. A white car grazed the left side of the car, taking the mirror with it. Horns were honking wildly, raining down on the terror of confusion as he kept turning the steering wildly back and forth with random madness, unable to take control. She saw the dump truck heading for the front end of the car, but in her heart she knew that if Mr. Curvil was her father, he would protect her, but if he was not, her father that was somewhere watching over her would protect her, because she was kind and obedient. So she closed her eyes and waited.

CHAPTER 6

Puppet in the Pulpit

"**H**ey, it's church time, wake up! Let's get busy, we've got a house to ruin."

"Shut up, I took the overnight watch. I'm tired."

A vicious blow connected his ear to the tree limb in which he was crouched.

Miserable profanity echoed loudly. "What was that for?"

"Your sacrilegious disrespectful attitude. You have a subtle way of letting me know you want to be in charge."

"In charge? I was just saying I worked last night, and I am tired."

"Get out of that warm crook of the tree. I'm on my way to blow an electrical fuse. Don't let me wait on you."

He raised his humongous black wings and swooped down to the parsonage below where Pastor Pippy and his wife were having the same fight. She was on her way to make the coffee, so he had to get to the fuse before she could get the pot started. There, he got it, done. Next, he slid through the walls into the kitchen quickly enough to kick the edge of the rug, to stage her fall. Great, on her face; that should set up a little bruise. She groaned, a weary kind of groan, the kind that could break your heart—if you had one. She turned over, sat on the floor, and wept.

Their lives were still on a roller coaster. It was Sunday morning, the day of worship, and her husband woke up with his excessive bickering over irrelevant trivialities that did not exist. Her value in this relationship had eroded a long time ago; she was just a front to keep his empire intact. In charge, he accused her of wanting to be in charge when all she said was, "I am tired." The tears began to well up in her eyes again, this time more of a question to God. When would He smile at her prayers? She indulged herself in her woes for a moment but heard David's footsteps coming; better pull herself together, nothing pleases him, but on the floor, crying, would be the perfect setting for his Sunday morning brawl. She scurried to fill the coffee pot with water and get the roast from the cupboard. He was there.

Fearful slid through the wall and stood tall beside her.

"What took you so long, loggerhead?" Control asked.

"The coffee hasn't started yet? What's taking so long?" her husband asked? He did not wait for an answer. "You have a bruise on your forehead."

"I have bruises everywhere," she muttered. She finished the setup and turned on the switch. Nothing happened. She reached for the plug. That was okay. Fearful slid behind her and whispered. "You know what will happen if you tell him, he will blow a fuse."

"Can you help me dear, this, this... I don't know?" her words were soft but timid.

"What is it?" He moved beside her and their bodies touched; it felt strange, repulsive, unappealing. She shrugged it off.

"You must have blown the fuse." He turned on a few other switches. "Typical of you, my dear. I'm going to get ready, I will get coffee at the church."

She watched him walk away. A chuckle rose in her chest. *I blew a fuse, I have powers, I am the best.* The chuckle bubbled into a knot. This day would need all the strength she could draw from the Lord.

Fearful rode in the back seat, but Control sat on the roof, he liked the extended view. From his pivotal point, he could see all the activities around, and with his powers, he manipulated a few, even though they were not his assignments. He just loved to stir up trouble.

"Hey Lust, what's going on? Where is your ring? You alone?"

"Just chilling, taking it easy today." The response was a blend of confidence with a cry for help.

He slid from the top of the roof to entertain the lonely geek. "Hey, talk to me, you are Lust, not Liar. What happened?"

"They kicked me out."

"What about your ring?"

"I got tired of them—they confused everything. The prince did not give me a good ring."

"Not to worry, I could use you. Just remember I don't take no muss—this post is tight." Lust grinned and rose at the offer. They flew to the church together.

Fearful got his chance to wield his influence. He would bond the two together and sabotage Control's work of misery.

"You know I love you?"

"Talking to me?"

"Yes, David, I really love you."

"I have not heard those words in forever."

"I would love to whisper them to you every day, not only the words, but I long for us to be gentle and loving again. I would love us to start over, erase the pain and the hurt, and begin loving each other like the days we first met."

"Angelique, too much has happened to go back to the past."

"We can erase the past!"

"We are not God."

"True, but we can wash the past clean with hearts of forgiveness." There was silence. "David, so much in our lives have evolved and made us successful, things we did not foresee at the beginning. However, we have embraced them to bring profit to our lives so we can continue to experience God's blessings as they flow. I believe that is the heart and the attitude we must apply to loving each other. We must embrace the mental and emotional development that facilitates our success yet harnesses the softer side of these attributes to understand and cherish the beauty we have in each other."

"Did you rehearse this?"

"David, I need your love to make me the best I can be. When I know your love is strong, it covers me like a cloak, and I am able to conquer anything. Without the strength of your love, my mind is weakened and I become emotionally drained trying to balance my unhappiness with all I have to do."

He reached his hand over and squeezed hers gently. It felt good.

"We should get away together, even for a weekend and reconnect again, you know, enjoy each other." He smiled. It touched her heart. He was different, strangely different.

"Yes, let's get away. How about next weekend? Book a trip, somewhere quiet, Thursday to Saturday." He raised her hand and kissed it.

Her heart raced. "I'll go shopping and pick out a few negligees you'll love."

"You are still my greatest treasure in life. Hon, sometimes I seem angry, but it's not you, it's just the pressure of the ministry, you understand."

She sighed and blew out the suffocating stench she had been holding onto for years. It lightened her soul and blew Fear right out of the back seat.

They pulled into the pastor's parking space and he reached over and kissed her gently, looking deep into her eyes and savoring her sweetness as never before. Control swooped down to the car door with Lust by his side, concerned about the little encounter he was witnessing. Pastor Pippy sensed the spirit and collected himself to start the business of the day. The church was bustling with people, and it made him feel powerful.

Control turned to Lust, "Make yourself useful, find your niche." He followed Pippy to his office.

What was that I just saw in the car?

Thoughts ran dreamily through Pastor Pippy's head. *Just for a moment I connected with Angelique again.*

That woman has served her time, she will destroy this empire if you continue to give in to her ruse.

But there is a sweetness about her that makes me powerful, even without all of this.

That power cannot bring you fame. The power you wield in this Church will propel you to your ultimate destiny. Think about it, she weakens you, that's not power.

But I am so much more secure in her love than when I taunt her. I feel despicable and ugly when I do, but with her by my side, I know I can conquer the world.

Gather your thoughts, that's not who you are. You are strong, you control everything, you don't need Delilah's help. Delilah is the knife in your back—that's the way it always is.

"Good morning Pastor David, I have your coffee." It was Martha, the secretary.

"Thank you, Martha."

"Are you ready to meet with the leaders now, Pastor?"

"Let me gather my thoughts. Have them ready in five minutes."

That's a beautiful girl, have you ever looked at her?

Martha is the backbone of this ministry, I won't muddle that water.

You said it, how much better it would be to gain control of her mind. Think of it. If Percy ever marries her, she will not serve you as she does, she will be divided between him and the ministry. But if you corner that mind and manipulate it, then you control her forever.

That's a great idea! Let me think, let me think. I've been distracted this morning, I can't afford that. Where is my sermon? I need more finances pouring in. Let me focus on that instead of these silly women. Women are for weak men.

Not at all! Women are for strong men who know how to harness their intuition to honor and serve them. Think about it! Seventy-five percent of this congregation are women, you can have these women opening up their husband's wallets for your benefit if you appeal to their delicate side. Here is what you should do. Make them see you as the perfect husband to Angelique, the kind that every woman dreams of, and you will have them eating out of your hand. Then, subtly suggest the need for financial growth, and they will open their bank accounts to do your bidding.

Not a bad idea!

In your sermon let the Church know you are taking Angelique on a weekend get-away to rekindle the fire you once had. It will take off the harsh edge, soften them up to you.

Enough, enough, let me focus on this sermon. I cannot afford to look like a fool up there. I must get my game face on.

"Pastor, the team is ready. They are waiting in the boardroom."

"Jesus Christ!" he muttered under his breath.

Bwaak, bwulk. Are you trying to drive me out of here. Do not use The Name.

Pippy was already out the door. Control had to go clean the vomit from his perfect attire.

Lust was making his rounds, but not making an impact. It was not because he had lost his touch: he was new to this environment and needed to establish bonds. This church was a mixed bag, plus the self-assured atmosphere made it extremely difficult to introduce himself. Very few weaklings attended this church, so there were no vulnerable needy preys, mourning from the loss of a broken heart or needing consolation beyond human capacity. The women were assertive control freaks who took charge of fundraising and prided themselves on the values they raked in. The men were golfing buddies and business partners who lived for the competition of raising up another conglomerate to stroke their egos. The young girls were programmed to expect the flabbergasting diamond as the token of belonging and that anything less meant their future of being the *creme-de-la-belle* was shattered forever. Of course, the boys were interested in playing the wild card, but that meant finding a floozy, and floozies did not tread these carpets. Uh, what control!

He would check the bathroom. The attention seekers are always touching up—that's where you find the insecure, those on the prowl.

Ugh, you are beautiful.

Indeed, I am stunning. Oh, my eye liner just smudged. Scott will notice—I know he has an eye for these things.

That could be your conversation line.

No, not at all. I cannot afford to look less than perfect.

Lust sighed. This place is full of control, he'd better leave.

Two seconds and whoosh, Control came through the glass with such force it knocked the eye pencil from Miss Gorgeous-prissy-proper. Served her right.

"Loser, I heard you over the sound of the music. I'm beginning to think you have no balls. I thought you had the easiest job of us all. I need to work out a few kinks with the lead singer, so I'll show you around in a bit. Everybody needs you from time to time, and I have secured a job for you in the office."

"Why the hell you calling me loser? I am here to help you. I don't tolerate disrespect. Wherever I go I am adored. One more damaging word out of you and I am gone."

"Ok, ok, here's the secret: in this environment you enter by force and manipulation. Create the need, duffle head. Where is Fear? Miss Gorgeous here could stand to be fearful of rejection while burning with lust. Get busy knuckle-head. You are so daft. I don't like weaklings on my team, here, take a bit of my power."

The wind of Control blew through Miss Gorgeous' ear and into Lust. She inhaled the fragrant air of confidence, picked up her purse, and headed off to find Scott.

The band struck up their synchronized note, and Control went to take his rightful place on the pulpit. Things looked good from his throne. Affluence, social stature, politicians, business moguls, all on time, all in place. He had wielded such a powerful reach, he could not help but puff a little. Pastor Pippy rose to address the audience, and he slipped inside of him.

Be confident, you do not need to prepare for who you are. Your sphere of influence reads like the gospels. Relax, you got them.

Pastor Pippy smiled with confidence and delivered the opening remarks of the century. *Whet my whistle, I am good.*

The band followed with its second hymn, right on time, and harmonious voices accompanied the sound as worship began.

"All hail the power of Jesus Name, let angels prostrate fall..."

He flinched, he twitched, he itched, then he snuck out of Pastor Pippy. He could not stand it. It was all because of that misguided lunatic Lust, whose insufficiency botched his influence. He was not able to complete his morning routine because he had to go see about the idiot's ranting.

Let me go find that fool. He knew lust had left the building because he could not feel him anywhere, plus, none of them could stick around for the kind of worship that exalted The Name. It tore them all apart.

As he soared through the air, it struck him that he had left his post. He would use the time to gather Lust and a few other idiots for his team. Plus, how could he go back when they were calling that Name. He would get this business settled and be back in time for the sermon.

As he soared through the air he was amazed to see the low frequency of evil on a Sunday morning, especially compared to the heat produced just a few hours before. Something had to be done; this was his town, he needed a bigger team. Fearful was useless in greater matters. He was only good at silencing Angelique's purpose and assignment; but, true to his nature, he could not get a stiff upper lip anywhere else.

He needed Lust and he could certainly benefit from Pride, then Rejection and Fear would be a good combination. Occasionally he could use Theft, but he would rather not have crime or prostitution, they were messy and he wanted a clean town. He must arm himself with a ring of obedient troopers. It was time to launch big. That kind of language in worship sent the quivering sickness that they could use his demise against him. What if they called for The Blood, that would ruin his kingdom.

"Lust," he bellowed. Nothing in sight. At the Old Fellows Hall a group was gambling for the right to manipulate the upcoming golf tournament. Lust would not be there. On second thought, he never knew what he could find. He swooped in.

"What brings you here Moron? Can't hold your turf on your big day?"

"See, I pity you, Gamble, you achieve only by the luck of the draw, and that's why you only attract the low-life's. Join my team and I guarantee success to the tenth degree. I can relieve you from the failure that has cloaked you like a perfume."

"Desperation is ringing loud and clear in your voice, oh pompous one. We all heard that song your church belted out onto the turf—got to be more careful Chief."

"Here's an idea, gather your ring and come join my team. These men could also join my church. Just remember who's in charge."

"What do I get in exchange?"

"I will map out those details after midnight. Take your thumb out of your mouth and get these boys to my church now."

"I don't trust you, but I will, and if I don't get what I want, I will blow your cover."

Control was out of ear shot: not really, just no more time for that halfwit. No one was working their joints on Sundays, huh? So many places were empty. Families were enjoying breakfast or sleeping.

A streak of maliciousness entered his space, and he turned to acknowledge the spirit he hated and dreaded. This thing had the power to sabotage hell.

"You called, my Lord." The sarcasm was loud.

The two halted in mid-air and Control tried to size up how to use the thing without capsizing his boat. The trouble with this kind was its unpredictability. He had worked too hard to have his empire fall into stupidity.

"I called for Lust." Control did not hide his disgust.

"Master, he is hiding. His balls turned to jello with just one moment in your presence. Your Highness, he works better with the rejects and the cowards. Now here is an excellent idea for our perfect partnership. I am perfect to stir up a little harmless trouble, and if I am guaranteed a secure place on your team, I will persuade Lust to be our lifelong partner. Deal?"

"Deal! You washed-up idiot, I would not make a deal with a traitor. Now, follow along and I will see about keeping you around." He shot through the air, his tail leaving a trail of soot. "Tell me, where is Perversion? With my affluence, I need a higher-classed bait than that knucklehead Lust."

"Master, two towns across is a massive ring. I'm sure they could spare you some of their best."

"Take me there. Where do you find time to know these things? Don't you have any purpose to attend to, any lives to ruin?"

Malice shot off in the distance using his seeming obedience as a deterrent to the answer. He knew Control had locked up the town, and all of them were quietly praying for a way to get in. This was their time and he was not going to blow the chance by trying to protect his ego. Let Control spout his insults, soon he would be put out of business, and this town would be a mess.

Business was booming in Loversburg. The joints were open and rings were everywhere, busy. The ambience of the town was in shambles, a disgrace to look at, but they all seemed delightfully satisfied in the mess. He would choose wisely, something with an eye for class, something that understood the subtlety of effecting a crippling sabotage while staying on top of the game, keeping things clean.

The environment jarred his nature—the main house was loose with brawls and squabbles, while twerps doubled over in corners reeling from overdoses. The stench of overnight vomit mixed with booze, men drunk with Lust and women tantalized with Low Self-esteem, served up a rich booming business cocktail. What a bag of worthless schmucks! He hated the idea that he had to rummage through this unskilled set of dimwits to establish more control. But his growth was outstanding, and he needed help to prevent those buffoons from calling on The Name he was sent to stomp out.

The doofus on karaoke sounded pretty good. That's it, how about a singer that could outdo them all, and of course, he had to cater for a little Witchcraft. A bit of dabbling thrown into the mix should lay to rest the use of sacrilegious songs in his church once and for all.

Malice interrupted his disapproving scan of the joint.

"Master, I have selected the finest of the lot, and they are ready at your beck and call. May I introduce to you the replacement for your worship leader and..."

"You heard me; you tapped my vision?"

"Master, I have given myself wholly to your service. I only tapped in to please you."

Control could strangle the twit. The tone was soothing, but something in his nerve told him it was as condescending as hell.

"Look, Master, you will be pleased with the beauty of Whoredom. She has the touch and the taste I know you desire. I thought that Prostitution was a bit outlandish—she attracts dejects, and places high demands—but this beauty, on the other hand, works for free, at your beck and call; and because of her desirous beauty, she will lure the unsuspecting into her nest without flaunt and flamboyancy, just the kind of high-valued privacy you desire for the town."

"Malice, you are good. What else you got?"

"Well, I have a treasure for you, but there is just a little flaw with singer-boy here; he is hooked on drugs. I tried, but I think with your control, and the affluence you will provide in his surroundings, in no time, he will become your slave."

Malice came closer to whisper. "His real problem is not Addiction. Addiction replaced Low Self-esteem a long time ago. This boy has no desire for the drug, so if placed in an ambience of confidence such as yours, he will thrive."

"Battle-cry! Pippy must need me." Control turned on his heel to twist out of sight, but the gentle hand of Malice restrained him with a nudge.

"Master, just before I met up with you, I saw Slumber, and I asked him to keep an eye on things till we got back."

"You fiddlehead, who are you? What's in this for you? How dare you interfere with my church? He grabbed the scrawny puppet by his throat, pulling tight to choke out the air. Looking into his eyes as he was suspended in the air, Control could detect nothing but malicious evil, so he shoved him back as he let go. There was something nauseating about this imp, something.

"Bring them to Bible Study this Wednesday. Stay out of my way—I have my eye on you."

He was swollen with anger and found it hard to maneuver his flight. He had to return hastily to church, but he felt unusually tired and sleepy. His wings got heavier with each push. He knew it, Slumber was in charge and preventing his return. Just before his bloated, sleepy frame hit the ground with a loud thud in the thicket below the Chapel de Chiens, he vowed to ring the scrawny neck of Malice and lay him to rest.

David and Angelique were sound asleep. Fear was not in the tree. Everything was peaceful. That was wrong. He wanted details of the church service, but Slumber had dipped out of town. He was embarrassed to go find that malicious grunt of a pig that hacked his day. His blood was alive with revenge; he had to double up on his mission.

Everyone in his rank was gathered for the reckoning session of the quarter. Reports were due and he was bloody good until yesterday. First, it was that stupid song; no, come to think of it, the trouble started by inviting Lust into his church. He would report on the slothfulness of idle imps and call for an order to imprison or punish those whose laziness create havoc.

"Church-boy, welcome, you are late." Disorder purposefully picked out a seat beside the lofty Control. "Everyone heard of your little snafu yesterday. I tell you rumors go fast and wild. Is it true you lost control to an upstart?"

He turned his head to respond, but the imp disappeared into a foul-smelling musk of powder. The roll call was issued, and he bowed with all the grace that was left in him.

Reports kept rolling in. He did not expect such a splendid report from Imprisonment, but apparently his turf was growing by the second. It was his turn.

"Master, I have victory to report. Your turf is safe and tightly controlled; all is functioning effectively. The numbers speak for themselves, and the town is in a headlock of control."

"You speak so assuredly, but your effectiveness needs be enhanced by that which stifles the truth and substitutes religion. Have you ever considered partnering with Lies or Religion or Deception? You may get more work done.

Next. Malice, your report please."

"Master, I have indeed been the spiteful little traitor that was created. I helped out Control yesterday, who failed in his primary duties. I reclaimed the town from the blessings that follow truth, by tucking the congregation quietly to sleep, then maliciously twisting the sermon to read that The Name of umm, the name Jesus has been so common throughout time that no one knew which "He-soos" they were calling on. After all, I inserted, it could be your neighbor from Brazil. The Church exploded in laughter and bought the theory, hook, line, and sinker. Master, I even had time to engage the pompous Control in a little rendezvous of intrigue while I kept him away from my assignment. Therefore, I have added another star to my crown. I must respectfully request that you add an adage of honor for my carefully crafted plan."

Control was stiflingly embarrassed. *So it was Malice who staged himself as Lust, no wonder he bumbled in his imitated influence. I tried to pour out my heart in generosity to the evil, while his malicious plot was to disrupt my turf? I know there is dissension in ranks, but this little upstart, I will get him chained for this.* He began to bloat again from excessive anger and had to control himself. He left the conference licking his wounds. He had no desire to return to Pippy; he needed some good advice. Prince Casino had a tight ship; the trip was imperative.

Lights were everywhere, the glitter of wealth shone up to high heaven, the city was teaming with life. That was the joke: teaming with life or teaming with death amid the glitter? Just outside the City he could see the rejects. Oh, he keeps the substitutes happy by facilitating a place for them just outside his turf. Lesson 101. Keep going, there is more to learn. It was approaching morning and Prince Casino should not be on guard, but everything flowed so naturally, he must be on the watch. He was spotted by a few big shots who knew he was an out-of-towner, but he kept going, desperate to view the lay of the land. The foulest activity ascended from the brothels, they were strategically positioned on every block and gave the

Prince his stripes. He perched on the tower of an old church to watch and learn. The stench of sin oozed up, but the air on the street was clean, so just passing by you could never sense the pleasurable horror that flowed on the inside. He counted the strikes, about three victims had gone already and a fourth was on his way out. But there was a hush about it so nothing would leak onto the street. A general sat on the top floor—he seemed to be the Lawyer, all jazzed up. The police had just arrived. Money was exchanging hands. Two of the victims would be discarded, they had no value. The other two had families, and so Deception had to be called in to work out a deal.

The casinos themselves were elegant testimonies of grace to hell. He could not build one of these, but he could sure run the church like one if he studied it carefully. Every floor, every room, was occupied with evil. Even the kitchen was being run by Glamour and Ruin. He would never have thought to place the two together, clever idea. Waste controlled the shops, and the floors were partying with opportunists. Each person that came through the doors was assigned a demon to escort them around and make them comfortable. Eventually, the demon shackled themselves to the minds and manipulated the actions—strategy to the max. This was the university of strategic management.

He was distracted by activity from the back door of the brothel two blocks from the church. The two bodies linked to families were being carted off, with Lawyer seated on the top of the ambulance. He turned to watch it leave. Lawyer hatched a plan with Deception: arrange accidents with both vehicles and pronounce them dead at the scene.

"I see you are here to learn; the curiosity of your peaked interest wafts across my turf for miles. How can I help you, my friend?" It was the Prince himself. He never looked more regal. He was escorted by Pride and Greed. Envy entered his heart just listening to him.

"Prince, how are you?" he condescended. "You have a thriving hell-hole right here on Earth."

"Business is business. But how can I help you?" The tone was not of the old pal he ran with years ago. The attitude was cocky and dismissive. He was determined to break through to his mind, for surely he did not have a heart.

"I am seeking someone to trust, a friend to give me advice."

Pride did not miss the opportunity. "A miserable failure is no good for my turf. It leaks into the infrastructure and spoils everything."

The Prince gloated at the sharp answer from his bodyguard. "Let's do this. Follow me to the edge of town. I cannot have your kind on my highest pinnacle."

"An impressive empire, Prince, it wreaks with every odor of hell, yet it is cunningly overlaid with the mesmerizing glitter that attracts all. I am impressed."

The praises were too much for Pride; his sword was down as his head reeled in the praises. Greed had held his tongue long enough, plus his ego needed to be stroked.

"It will cost you."

"I am sure."

The stench from the outskirts of town drowned out the conversation as they all began coughing. They swerved and followed the path of the river.

"I want Pippy as ransom."

"Oh, Prince, he is my greatest asset."

"You are weak. In a town that large, your fingers should be in every pie. Your problem is control; you want too much control so there is no gut-wrenching sin in the town. You cannot build on control: to become successful you must build on sin; you need some slime balls."

"I can't give up Pippy—that would shatter the town, and everything would fall apart."

"You are wasting my time."

"How about Angelique?"

"She is of no use to me; she has a bond to His Blood. I cannot penetrate that. Tell you what, I'll send my boys in and stage a major bloodshed, then I will spare you a few good talent."

"May I keep them?"

"After the bloodshed they are yours."

"Will I keep Pippy?"

"Yes, you can. Be off, your turf is bleeding."

He had compromised with a deal that made no sense. He needed some time to think; he could not go back to the next reckoning looking like a wimp, it was against his nature. He admired the Prince, but his strategy was ruthless. He had no heart. That's it, that was the answer; rule to destroy, do not rule with compassion. So that little peabrain of Fear was a defect as a bodyguard. He decided to perch on a loft just outside the next town. He must make a plan. He knew Angelique was an intercessor, but so far, it did not interfere with his plans. As a faithful little Christian, she submitted herself to her husband and did not usurp his authority. As long as he had the greater influence over Pippy, she was just a back-up player. The Prince did not want her dead; that was strange. Now he had to ramp up the town's evil, but he trusted no one help him. He hated giving up control. He would take two more days before he went back to Londonsville and Pippy, his puppet. He needed to see other turfs; perhaps he could learn more.

"Master, wake up, disaster has struck our town, and I am afraid. I don't know what to do."

"Fear, you look horrible."

"The angels came in, I tried to fight but they were huge. I even got an ear chopped off."

"How much damage?"

"Major. Light is bursting from every home, and prayers are rising. Master you have been gone for two weeks, I'm not sure we have a place there anymore."

"Nonsense, get out of my way. I'll take it back. Pippy and the town belongs to me."

"Master, Angelique took David to The Blood; they took the sacrament together, and he confessed, he repented. They pray together now, they are happy. I cannot even find a hole to enter the house. They found Love. They asked for angels with drawn swords to guard the house, and the Church is having a prayer vigil starting tonight to bring angelic reinforcement to the town. Governor Bell called his staff to prayer this morning and petitioned for The Blood."

"Shush, you fearful piece of trash. Do not fill my ears with that holy talk." Control tried to rise up from his comfort of slumber but felt the webs of spiritual chains. He tried not to let Fear see his dilemma. "Who is the lead angel?"

"I don't know, Sir. I got beaten up so badly, I ran for my life. I've been searching for you for days. I met up with Gamble, and he said there was a plea to cast you out and keep you bound."

"Follow me." He struggled to raise himself, aching from every joint. He was not able to lift himself.

"Fearful, I need strength. Give me some of yours so we can go get reinforcement."

Fear had heard the sweetest compliment of his life, and without thinking he slipped into Control and they took off. The sun was setting and Prince Casino's turf was inviting; the sights of evil strengthened his limbs.

"Get out of me Fear, I can do it now."

As they entered the town, a gang of four met them in flight. "How can we help you?" It was Anger, he had an Italian accent. Control couldn't be sure if he was Italian or if it was just boastful play.

"I need audience with the Prince."

"He sent us to meet you and ask that you stay on the outskirts of town. You know, you don't smell too good." The Italian accent carried a mocking tone, but Control knew that the smell of defeat was all over him.

"Can I talk with him? We have a deal. I am here to sure it up."

"We can help."

"I need reinforcement for my town. Things have gone sour."

The beasts burst out in hysterical laughter. "You've got to be the greatest loser of all times." There was more roaring laughter.

"My friend, that will cost you some more." It was Greed, the slime ball.

"How much?"

The Italian spoke, "I don't know, I have not accessed the damage. Let's just say, if we take the town, it belongs to us."

Control reeled. Impulsive bastards! He hated them already. "The Prince, can I talk with him?"

"He has no time for losers, my friend, we are all you have. Oh, let me introduce myself: I am Rebellion, if anyone can redeem your town, I can. Let's settle it now. Give over your keys and follow my lead."

Where would he go, what did he have now? He could give up his rank and reside in the town as a shove-around or go back alone to fight and face his disgrace. "How large a ring are you taking for the fight?"

"Oh, I have lots of dejects that are waiting to be used. Hand over the keys, I'll take the lead."

Control reached up to the chain over his heart to get the keys. They were not there. He looked. They were gone. Shock waves ran through his body. They had stolen the keys by prayer. It was not theirs, how dare they? His blood began to boil.

The foursome broke out in hysteria. The laughter attracted a host of dejects. Soon, the whole crowd was laughing. He had lost everything. He knew it.

Just one day of entertaining the disguised Malice, and the empire crumbled.

"I know the town, I can help restore it to our Commander." He desperately wanted to be part of the coup, at least then he could retain some position.

"You can tag along, but we don't need you. That's now open target, and whoever stakes claim, wins." They were off.

"Let's steal some of their dejects with the bribery of rank and position, then let's form our own coup and fight from a different angle—not trying to defeat the angels, but sneaking in through windows and basements, destroying from the inside out. We know where to go and who will let us in. Master, gather your own team and control them. Lay out the plan, we can do it."

He gazed at Fear—never thought he had the guts, but he was right. The idea was worth everything.

The town was beaming with holy light mostly radiating from Pippy's cathedral. Little pockets of fire were burning on the rooftops of homes. They dared not enter those, the Holy Spirit was there. His first order of business was Pippy. It was dark and he could see the glistening swords, but the angels were invisible. They stood watch at the four corners of his land, and a covering made it impossible to see on the inside. He sailed over to the church. He had to take the long route, angels were everywhere, prepared for war.

He could hear the prayers. What in the name of Jezebel could reclaim a town in such a short time? Two weeks and righteousness was exalted to this level, unheard of. Some unsuspecting soul must have been praying all along. That's it, search for the source of prayer. No, no time for that. Every deject and his brother knew the town was up for grabs, so there was no telling who would be fighting and what evil strategy they would engage to lay their hands on a position of this magnitude. Stomping out the prayer would make it easy for the power-grabbers to win. He was in the business of desecrating his enemies, not empowering them. Let them fall into the traps of the chains of prayer.

"Fearful, go get help from Loversville. Promise them free access anytime, once we clean up this mess."

"Yes, sir, I'll get all I can. Bribery, ride with me—we can do well together."

Control turned to look at the trail of imps that had followed him. He didn't like them and he didn't trust them, but this was not the time to indulge his nature. He would issue their assignments and let them fail or succeed. It did not matter—the better ones would prove themselves, others would get slain and run out of town. One by one, he issued their assignment according to their name. Impotent was next in line.

"What role can you play in battle? Aren't you low down and good for nothing?" He wished he hadn't said it but the words were out already. The thing looked so pathetic, yes, it looked impotent.

"I, Sir, will weaken the hearts of the greatest prayer teams in this town. Just show me the backdoor to that church."

Talk about underestimating a soldier. Control smiled. "John, the janitor, at Sixty-six Quiper Lane does not like Pippy, so he's your man." The thing shot off in the distance.

Control was getting weary, the same weariness that put him to sleep back in Tridesvale. He needed a body or an imp to rejuvenate his strength. This was indeed warfare. In his fifty years of this town, he had never seen this, nor had he seen it coming.

The host of demons waiting on their instructions burst into flames as a sword gnashed and twisted through the crowd. He rolled backward but the tip burrowed through his right knee. The massive angel pivoted him in the air while twisting the heavy weapon. He tried to free himself, but the man had him tagged. He was already weak, this was not a fair fight. A swift streak of light burst around him, and blackness surrounded his soul.

"Master, I stole some blood for you; you must regain your strength. Here, Sir, have some." The fragile wimp of Fear tried to prop up his master.

"Rattlesnakes!" A string of profanity rang through the heavens from the lips of the wounded Control. "My knee, my knee."

Fear was sympathetic. "This will help you heal, Sir."

He looked at the thing with kind eyes. Fear was his name, and loyalty was his game. He stifled the pain and reveled in the attention. It was young blood, pure blood, the good kind. "How did you manage this? I tricked a man in his dream into fearing for his life, he took his child while sleep walking." Fear smiled.

"You are worth keeping. How is Londonsville, and how did you find me?"

"I belong to you, Sir, it is my business to help you. Someday I will be as great as you are, but right now I can be of the most help by serving you." He attended to his idol and master. "Master, the ring from Loversville did not buy in on the deal. They were content on being dejects, no ambition to rise. So I went to Wenchtown and got a few workers from there. Everyone knows what has happened, some have decided to help us fight."

"I have a second flagon of blood, Sir. This one will fix you right up, and I am truly ashamed of how I got this one, so please do not ask."

Control enjoyed the blood. It excited his soul and life flowed into him.

"Let's not go yet, Master. Prince Casino's team is fighting now. I suggest we go recruiting the team we always wanted."

"David."

"Yes, dear."

"I had a dream last night. In the dream I was the mother of two wonderful boys. I was sleeping by my husband and black smoke began to fill the house as if it were on fire. My husband jumped up to go see the boys, but he was clobbered over his head and fell to the floor as dead. Then he rose up growling; he had become a monster. He grabbed my body and hurled me out of the house, through the wall as if it were invisible. I could not control myself; I was being tossed through the air for miles. But while going through the air, my husband went through town killing babies and collecting their blood."

David turned white as a ghost. "Let's pray."

Jesus Christ, Son of the living God, avenge the blood of your children. We bind up the monster that steals our children, in the name of Jesus Christ; cripple every activity of darkness and confuse their plans. I speak dissension to the ranks of darkness. I speak power to the angels with drawn swords to locate and destroy every work of darkness. We debilitate the strength of the enemy and call forth the saints to cry out to the living God for mercy. Forgive our sins, Lord, and heal our land. Every work of darkness will be sabotaged and crumbled by the blood of Jesus Christ. Amen.

Honey, hurry call up the leaders and let's meet for prayer and communion at the church in an hour. I will call John the janitor as well, I want to pray with him.

Let's start a mandatory prayer chain with any church for fifty miles that will pray and fast with us. We are in warfare for our lives."

CHAPTER 7

Losing Ground

"**M**amma, I need you. I need you, Mamma, tell me how to do this. I'm losing, losing, losing everything."

She held tightly on to the frail hands, shaking them with urgency. "I know you can hear me, talk to me, help me please."

Her sobs caused the old crone to raise her head. Her eyes were old—the lids had lost their tone and folded lazily on top of the vivid lashes. The strong jawbone was no longer graced with the glow of plump flesh, but thin lines dragged themselves to connect with the curved chin. Her hair had kept its volume, but it sat about her face like a dirty mop that was wrung and set to dry. It was not a pretty sight.

She lowered her face onto her mother's lap, preferring not to be distracted by the bewitching looks. Her tears felt warm on the smelly cotton. Slowly, the cold bony hands stroked her head in sympathy.

"It is a precarious tight rope walk of tragedy." The shaky voice paused. "You must fine-tune the art of giving and taking. Do not take more than you give, and do not give more than you take—the price is poison to the soul."

She raised her head to capture the magic of the wisdom she thought was lost. She hadn't heard her mother articulate so fluently in years.

"Prepare your heart to make only the offers you need, the greater the offer, the deeper the bounty. Retreat is as fatal as indebtedness, yet the deeper you go, the greater the debt."

Her wobbling knees could no longer support her stoop. She lowered herself from her mother's lap to look into the face of a woman she had given over to be erased from the Earth by time. Her soul was alive, her heart was beating; how could she have missed out on the wisdom of this precious witch.

"I went too far, and then I died." It was a remorseful response, something that should have triggered tears, but her eyes were far away.

"What did you do?"

"Margo was my closest friend. We went to the same schools, worked at the same jobs, lived together for years until we got married. Neither of us was in love, we only wanted children, so we made ourselves available to the first men that showed interest. It wasn't long before we realized the bitterness our choices, but we had each other. Margo's husband was jealous of our relationship and punished her for it. Part of it was the joy he found in raping her, demanding that she produce children every year. Each time she conceived, she would come to me for help, and I would take care of the pregnancy. Finally, she carried a boy and found that it made her husband happy; but soon after the baby was born, he began to strangle and mutilate her mercilessly again, enjoying her half-dead body for his pleasure. She tolerated the abuse for seven years, then we hatched a plot. I called up Norion, he granted us secrecy and protection, if we would give him the boy. We did. Manny has never been the same."

"Mamma, I know him. He wants me, he is calling me to the other side. I trusted him to protect me too, but he has turned, torturing and demanding and furious. What must I do?"

"Adia, you gave the ultimate sacrifice when you stole the virtue of that man you went to in the country. You have not given a gift like that since."

"How do you know about it? Mamma, Mamma, how do you know?"

"You mentioned the affair with the man at Pickles when you came home, but that was the beginning of your fame in the city. You had to have taken a virgin."

"I found another man, a clean man. He had a wife, but he was clean. The seduction did not satisfy Norion, he wanted more. On the evening I planned the sacrifice, everything went wrong. Everything! So many of them were there waiting to have him. When the hour came, they taunted my soul in punishment, mangling and inoculating my mind until I passed out from the torment. I woke up days later only knowing that everything went wrong. I am so afraid to call him. I know he saw me but I do not know much of what happened."

"Have you appealed for mercy?" She did not wait for the answer. "Come with me."

Her creaking bones were louder than the rusted hinges of the old rocker. After several attempts to get out of the chair, she bowed herself, rose up, and ambled to the parlor.

The ritual was majestic. She could not remember her mother so illuminated in the ritual. Flawlessly, like the lines of a favorite song, the chants rang out.

"Adia, sing with me. It will grant you safety."

She joined in the chants, desperate for relief. Her mother reached for the smelly old mantle, straightened herself, and covered her daughter. The musty ancestral patchwork never smelled so good. She let the prejudice fade from her mind and settled to the floor as her mother weaved the protection she needed.

A delightful aroma wafted into her senses as her eyes fluttered to the light streaming into the parlor. It could not be. Did she sleep the entire night on the parlor floor? Breakfast! Her mother was making her favorite scones. Her body felt alive, and energy coursed through her soul. It was going to be a great day.

"Adia, you look radiant. Your energy is infectious. I confirmed your ten o'clock with Mr. Emills and a one o'clock with Mr. Langly, and that's it for your day. However, I want you to take a look at a resume I placed on your desk. She looks great and I thought I could use her in readings. Our client list is overflowing."

"Thanks, Maggi. I will be ready for Rich. Take him in when he arrives." Radiant! That was the energy of connecting her soul to the stored strength within her mother and the potent spirits of her generations passed on. The parlor truly carried a sacred aura. As she entered her office, she could also feel the glowing sensation all around her. She walked to the window and looked over the town she controlled. How wonderful it was to see her mother come alive, and come to her rescue.

Even though her mother had chosen a life of seclusion, her eagle vision penetrated even the stories she kept hidden. How much more does she know?

She never asked about marriage or having children. Perhaps she thought they were unnecessary. But how could a woman who loved her friend so deeply use her husband as a pawn?

Now she understood her father's distance, and just like her father had disappeared from her life, so she disappeared from relationships. Relationships felt like an indulgence that did not hold her soul. In fact, the few relationships she established were designed to gain magical powers, and after they served their purposes, she was on her way. Subconsciously, they were tied to her father, not only her father, but also her mother. Her passion in life kept her in love with her gifting, and every relationship was used to enhance its growth. However, deep in her soul, she wanted nothing more of abandonment or rejection, her father's disdain was all she could handle.

The breakup must have come when her father discovered her mother's magical powers; that must have been the way her mother gained entrance to his heart, for she never loved him. Poor man. She had erased his face from her heart, but today she wished to hear his story. He was the reason she never loved–well that and her friend. Her friendships infuriated him and he drove them away with his dirty tricks. Now he had turned on her, calling her, troubling her soul. But Mamma took care of that last night.

Confidence surged through her veins. How could she have overlooked the importance of her mother's abilities? How could she not see the characteristic of wisdom? How did she come this far without her mother's help? Laughter bubbled softly from beneath her breath as she reveled in the comfort of the protection weaved over her soul, a strong fort of protection generationally fortified. She closed her eyes and let her spirit drift off, off, away.

"Adia, you are a gift from Heaven, a treasure to be discovered in the Earth. I am here for you, I am your protection, I am your God."

The knock on the door was persistent. "Adia, Mr. Emills is here. I will give you a few minutes."

She was on the floor, collapsed in a bundle. What was that? The knock on the door interrupted her vision. The purest most comforting voice spoke so clearly to her. It must be a new chapter in her life. It was the protection her mother secured last night. She collected her vials, checked her face in the mirror, and headed to the Lavender Suite.

The cauldron boiled gently with the smell of lavender, which mingled with the smoke of the incense burning behind the curtains. Through the flickering light of the small candle, she could detect the unrest on Richard's face. By far, he was one of her best clients, a dark and devious lawyer whose soul was distressed by his path to power and his obsession for more. He trusted her completely and surrendered his soul to gain the wealth he desired.

Before she could get to her chair, the chimes started rattling. Norion was there. Lately, he was such a bull. She wanted someone else, someone like the tender voice she connected with just a moment ago. She took control.

"Be still, his soul is aching. Be still and let him weep for the dead."

The rattling stopped. Richard spread his hands across the small round table and bowed his head. She had trained him well. Be respectful to the soul of the one on whom you will climb to the next level.

After his penitence, she asked, "What will you have today?"

"She is five years old, it will seal every dream and define my glory. I want it to be my last gift, so I have come for your blessing and blessings from the dead."

She reached for the ball. Her hands hovered over the globe, her fingers mystically pulling at the shrine for answers. "I see a car, a truck, I see purity, innocence. I see a French door, I see a bul—... a buc, a bucket of water. There is water washing the marble floors."

She was glad he could not see her fright. She had to lie, and she needed to leave.

"Norion, Norion, speak. Tell us the future."

A rush of air swept through the room, and instantly the candle went out. There was silence.

She fumbled in the dark for one of her vials. She searched for his hand and clasped it shut, leaving the vial in his grasp. "Pour a drop three times per day on your feet for your protection." Bewildered, she sat for a moment then tapped on the bell for her assistant to escort him out.

It was almost time for her next client, but she had not regained her composure. Norion had confirmed her reading—there was trouble brewing in her client's life—but why should she make it personal? She really needed to focus on the voice, the pure voice she heard this morning. This was certainly a new day. She must learn to harness such spirits—it was good for business. Tonight she would spend some time reflecting on it and see where it would take her, but now she must head back to the Lavender Room.

He was not a handsome man. In fact, he was painfully ugly. What good had life offered to this poor man? On the contrary, he was a kind soul. He always brought in a gift for her and left generous tips for the staff, but today he seemed troubled, extremely troubled.

He bowed as he entered, "Madame, how are you today?" He laid an oval shaped gift, wrapped in pink satin with a pink polka-dot bow on the table. His hands were coarse and his nails unkempt—he truly was an unattractive package. She looked into his eyes and saw a hole so deep, it was endless. "This gift you will enjoy for years to come."

There was something uncomfortable about his energy; even the gift sitting on top of the table oozed with the aura of misfortune. She lowered her head to mask the smirk on her face, thankful for the low light, wishing it could hide the anxiety in her voice. "Mr. Langly, you are indeed a generous man, thank you. What is your desire today?"

"My dream is that the most beautiful woman in the world would take my heart and make it hers."

"I cannot tamper with love. It is a gift of the gods."

"Then may I propose that you accept, unless of course, you have been given to another?" It was more of a question.

"The latter is true. Many moons ago, I was smitten and I have not looked back."

She was uncomfortable with the trend of the conversation. He had been her client for years, and had certainly gained her trust, but how daring to solicit her in courtship at a reading.

She pulled out the crystal ball and waved her hand around it, drowning out the present and asking for answers. Her chants flowed naturally, but her hands felt like they were bleeding. She knew well to follow the path of the ball, but the pain was unbearable and began to be released in her chant, a cry, a wailing pain.

Mr. Langly sensed it. "I don't need to know anymore." His voice was chillingly bitter.

"What do you know?"

"I know that life deals its hand of fate as it wills, and we are left in its cauldron to smother until the end. While some seem to have pleasured themselves with its goods, and to the untrained eye they bask in its beauty, a closer look reveals the misery and pain that surrounds their soul. I was not given the best of anything, not the smartest in the class, not the fastest on the team, not the most handsome in the room. I have learned to take care of myself throughout adverse encounters. Pain and regrets have paved my steps through much of my life."

His tone was sad and pathetic. He was lying, building his case for her sympathy.

"I want an easy life for once. I want you to tell me how to make my life beautiful. No more trauma or regrets, or being stepped on or being shoved aside, because someone better was chosen; no more being the footstool and the cleaner of the mess. Make me over. You can do it: give me your magic powers, fix me."

His curved palms strangled the air between them as they bobbed up and down to enforce his demand. His anger spouted from a mouth full of spittle that spilled to the sides of his lips without his notice.

"You did not come to me, Mr. Langly, you came here to be guided to your destiny. Magical powers do not supply demands, we are the puppets of a spiritual world to which we have sold our souls. What have you given in return for your demand? What is your offering? What are you willing to lose? What are you giving in exchange for your soul?"

The ridges of his jaws softened.

"The gods owe you nothing. Place your stake and pay the price, but be careful, very careful, and be ready to pay with your life."

She raised herself gracefully to conceal her jitters, tapped the bell, and exited the door in a hurry.

"Home early!" Her mother's voice was light and cheery.

Dinner smelled fabulous. The day had continued to reveal its countless surprises—there had to be a rush of activities in the sphere. Her mother was donned in a fabulous blue dress, with matching jade and sapphire necklace and earrings. Her hair was radiant with its sheen, curls falling softly to her bosom. She was smiling, the dazed and dreamy smile of a girl that had found love.

"Mamma, Mamma, you look mythical, transformed, amazing!"

"Thank you, dear. It has been a day of charming beauty. Hurry, get dressed for dinner—your father is on his way."

Her knees wobbled and clunked each other while hot air frolicked in a cyclone around her head. The last thing she felt was the ache of her twisted legs and the sharp pain inside her chest.

CHAPTER 8

The Last Drink

"Good evening, Mr. Emills, the gentlemen are meeting in the Roosevelt Manor. Enjoy your evening."

The country club was fairly quiet this evening, with only a handful of ladies at the pool. It could not be that they were losing money, not when he was about to become part owner. He wasn't satisfied with the offer. Instead, he felt like he was the sacrifice. These men wanted blood, and they were milking him dry. Curvil alone got over fifteen thousand dollars just to ensure a smooth delivery of the package. Resentment began boiling on the inside. Absolutely, he would demand more.

His hands were shaking as he grabbed the gold knob of the French door; he could see the rich snobs with their dirty smiles cavorting at the bar. He straightened his back and slipped into character. The greetings were loud and cheerful, as each man acknowledged his arrival.

"Rich, we've been waiting on you."

He wished he had a dagger for each eye, that would have been the perfect retort. "Great, great! What are you drinking?"

"Scotch and tonic."

"Let me have a Martini."

"Todd went down to his desk to fetch the contract for the club."

Tom assumed the role of boss in everything. He was president of the board of a financial holdings group and lived his life giving instructions. Todd was the president of the country club and the face behind the order. Bill was a superior court judge whose business was to provide clientele, and Jack, the president of a network of health services with various hospitals and insurance companies, supplied vital services and cover-ups, which kept the team alive.

"My wife is demanding that I take her to the game tonight—she has high stakes on the Bently's. The loser pays for the Aspen trip in January."

"My kids have been rooting for the Nippers, and I'll lay my bet they are going to win."

"Careful, Tom, don't let your wife get close to the boys on that team; you could have strong competition."

"What I lack in prowess, I supply in charm and money. I will not be outdone." Confidence beamed on his face as he downed his Scotch.

"Bill, you never got married: what's the story? Afraid? There was a pause. "Afraid of?"

"I have women eating out of my hands every day, swooning and catering to my every need. Why would I jeopardize that with jealousy?"

Todd walked in. "Smart. He would be the one signing his own divorce certificate."

Todd waved his hand and dismissed the bartender. The man nodded and exited the room.

Tom took the lead again. "Well, guys we have another ceremony scheduled for tomorrow. We will meet at eight to sign off on the documents. Todd, hand me the proposals."

Todd handed him a package and distributed papers to the rest of them.

"Jack and Rich will become part owners of the club, and the building at 696 Main has been purchased. Rich, we will hand that over to you tomorrow, just read and sign." He handed a stack of papers to Rich. "Bill, you were able establish closing yesterday, correct?

"As planned. There were a few glitches, but they got sorted out. The purchase agreement for Rich should be in your package."

He turned to Jack. "What was the highest bid?"

"Six million."

"Great, Jack, thanks that was good work."

Rich piped up. "Jack did not make that bid; it came from our firm. Emills and Offlin secured that bid against other investors."

Tom looked puzzled.

"I asked Rich to step in for me. I had to be out of town. Thanks, Rich."

Judge William blew out the flames. "The documents have been secured. Let us proceed."

"Todd, have the grounds been covered for tomorrow?"

"Certainly, the club is emptying out tonight, and will be closed through the weekend. Langly the janitor is on hand, and he has been well compensated. The room is ready for Curvil and his guest. We have also hoisted a few masts on the grounds for additional privacy. Everything is ready."

"Rich, when is Curvil expected?"

"He left this morning. He should have been here already."

Todd piped up, "I checked with Langly just before I came up. He had not arrived yet."

There was a nervous excitement of silence about the room. All eyes focused on Rich.

"We have been working the plot for months. The feedback was good. Curvil had begun dropping off and picking up from school, and that has been going smoothly. The mother stopped going to Raff-Taff and her other friends were discouraged from visiting the house, so she has been isolated for over a month. Curvil's been faithful to the plan, there is no need to worry."

Bill took the case again and deflected the heat. "The father has been sent away on six life sentences, so I don't think the child knows him. Last I heard, he had been isolated on a top floor cell and kept there for a while due to deplorable behavior."

"Richard, all reports are due today; you are making me nervous. Call Curvil."

Richard pushed back his chair to tend to the order, then said, "This is my third delivery, do not question my judgement. Curvil will be here."

The color in Tom's face was louder than his words. "It is now three o'clock. We will reconvene at six, and you better have that girl here by six."

"Gentlemen, your rooms are ready for the night. Let's push dinner back to seven." Todd wanted to show his diligence.

"I've got to take Camile to the games. Cancel my room, please, but I'll see you at six."

"Cancel mine too. I promised the family dinner tonight." Jack always had family plans.

Rich left the room, without a word. He was angry. He must calm himself and think of a way to destroy these imbeciles. He did not trust any of them. He would destroy them all. He would take Jack first, buy out his position as president by coercing him to spend more time with his family. Once he got the company, then Curvil could take him out. Then he would plan for Tom's wife, she was a putz for flirtation. Curvil couldn't handle that, he needed someone like Gart, who had some muscles. Take her to the edge of town, peg her, then send Tom to find her. See how much tough talk he would have then.

The phone kept ringing. Where was Curvil? It was eating at his nerves. He needed a drink. He rattled the handle of his car door before it dawned on him he had set out to go to his room. He jumped into the car and sped off with profanities oozing from his lips like the exhaust from his tailpipe. He called again. No answer.

It could not go wrong, not at the last minute. It made him look weak and pathetic, like an outsider trying to fit in. Only two more buildings, and Main Street would be his. He was not going to blow it.

The adrenaline rush from the ninety-five-mile-per-hour drive began to help him clear his head. He had to reclaim his pride tonight.

No one would show sympathy if Curvil and the child did not show up, not even Bill. There was a black hole where his heart used to be, filled with the blood of every innocent victim he had sentenced to death. That was where he enjoyed his first meal every day, beside himself, enjoying the torment of innocent blood.

He had always had cases in his court room, the typical run of the mill, who shot whom, who got justice, provide the evidence kind of story. But one day Judge William Wildly summoned him to his office for a little chat.

"You are a very ambitious man, Counselor, and it is duly noted that your firm is making generous strides here in the city. It is clear that your team of lawyers and investigators are ruthless and meticulous, leaving no room for doubt and error."

"Your Honor, I am sure you did not invite me into your chambers to lavish my firm with compliments."

"Correct, Richard. My request is notably delayed. However, the observed compliment is the very reason I have chosen you. There is a collaboration of corporate minds who have devoted themselves to the accumulation and manipulation of wealth. You would make an excellent partner."

"And beyond the excitement of this chess move?"

"You let me have my court room and in turn I will guarantee you and your firm the rise of success you dreamed. Mr. Emills, I want this case. The evidence in your portfolio must disappear."

The partnership was easy. The cases Bill wanted, he got, and Emills and Offlin filled a five-story building in the city in less than two years. The offer increased as properties came available, and soon an asset management group was added to the company.

When he joined the team, there were seven men. In the past two years, two had disappeared, and there were no questions asked and no answers supplied.

There just seemed to be more wealth to go around. Bob had gotten greedy, with frequent outbursts of rage when naming his loot. He made everyone insecure. Jim was old and forgetful and talked too much. He learned much of the history from listening to Jim. He must have stored the fatalities in his mind until they started speaking. You did not need to ask, he would tell. On a round of golf with the sherif and his out of town guests, Jim offered key evidence of transferred property and its deceased owners. Tom suffered a mild heart attack from the incident. The day Tom was released from the hospital, was the day of Jim's funeral. They did not tolerate internal errors, and everyone knew it.

He pulled up to his office. Curvil's car was not there. The office staff had left for the weekend and there were no messages on his desk or on his phone. He walked to the window then checked the time. His feet were visibly shaking, his heart was racing. It would be dark soon, perhaps he could go grab a junkie. No, they were picky—they wanted innocence.

"Tom, that's it, Tom!" The words were scarcely breathed from his lips when his heart settled back into its cradle and a wave of mocking peace washed his brow with beads of water. His feet rushed to the corner bookshelf, his hands so excited he had to consciously steady himself. He pushed back the books and revealed the safe. His brain waves were toxic with excitement, but after three lock-outs, he finally opened it. He reached in and retrieved the keys from the red envelope. He hadn't used it in a while. He closed the masterpiece and hastened to the basement. Bells of tantalizing joy swirled in his head; before they could think of laying a finger on him, he would take care of them all. Heck, Todd should also taste the brew of fate, and he could alter the club's papers to read "Property of Emills and Offlin." Keep Bill on for a few more days to legitimize the transactions, then lay his heartless soul to rest. Jack was no threat: he would dissolve the partnership and control the wealth.

In no time he was on the road headed back to meet his enemies. They had prepared the table and he had prepared the spread.

He wanted to find Langly before he went in. Langly kept more secrets than the grave. He was nowhere in sight. The marble tiles shone with the lights reflected from the wall sconces, causing his shadow to dance in patterns as he passed by. The elevator had never been so silent; an eerie tone raised it to the Roosevelt Manor.

The room was empty. He felt in his pockets; the pills were there. Great, why not make the drinks and wait for his friends. A smile graced his face as he strutted to the bar. The door opened behind him. It was Langly. Just the person he wanted to see. He saw the barrel and the bullet; he struggled, cried out in anguish and hit the floor.

CHAPTER 9

Destroy the Evidence

"**G**enerals, you have been summoned to this meeting as disturbing news has reached my ears. As bloodsucking leaders of territories and governing authorities, your failure is insufferable. Diabolical savages and ruthless murderers, addicts and molesters whose minds were twisted, sadistically programmed to serve up lifeless corpses and suicidal preys to my door, have become victims of the Bible.

That book is more widely distributed than it has ever been, and that must come to an end—too many are discovering the life in it. We cannot survive without blood, mortal blood, and your loss has begun to send hemorrhaging shocks through the realms of darkness."

"Commander, my Western territory is securely controlled. Regimes authorize strict adherence to contaminated religious theories with an official ban, imprisonment, or death, for those who use The Book."

"How effective is your security when I see light shining from your turf? Truth infiltrated your political system to create your demise. They were not stopped."

"Remember, Sir, before you gave me jurisdiction back in the 18th century the Catholics, Methodists, and Presbyterians laid grass root foundations that have been strongholds ever since."

"Commander, I have better news. In one state of the Eastern Corridor I have secured its ban after conjuring up verbiage from The Book itself to insinuate insults to the people. Those chosen to be used as the source of truth, the bearer of holy laws, and the initial carriers of the character of the one we fight against are discriminated against as racist. Race, I must add, is a strategic concoction of mine, designed to divide and conquer. Slight differences in physical appearances now separate their hearts in torturous friction. Division is alive and conquering is eminent. Master, we are on target."

"General, you are shortsighted indeed. While effectively stirring up a fluff about The Book, you gave it credibility on two counts. The ban is a facade because it generated interest and did not put an end to individual use. Next, you have now butchered centuries of covert craftiness by pinpointing the effectiveness of the crucifixion to a race we kept blinded. You are furiously overturning our plot."

"Sir, how about the lie that 'love your neighbor as yourself' advocates extra-marital sex and 'love your brother' purports incest?"

"Nonsense, General, no one believes it, not even you. The intention of a lie is that it becomes irrefutable, and even with research it still holds its soul. If you do not believe your lies, no one will."

"Commander, I have the best yet. I have seared the consciences of many missionaries, and twisted their passions to serve me by inveigling them to smuggle Bibles into tightly held countries with the lie that they are serving Him. I have emboldened them to break national laws regarding The Book that gets them thrown into prison. Some have been executed, others heavily fined, and most continue their illegal activity oblivious to the truth of the very word they advocate."

"Friend, a detour is not a change of direction. If the Word is preached, the Word takes effect. Can you recall where it was preached by a donkey?"

"Commander, I have instituted an order that supersedes all. I have established cultish orders, similar to the truth of the Anointed One, to corrupt the teaching and printing of the Book. To these cults I have attracted the most influential and authoritative minds, blinded so effectively, they write their own laws and desecrate the truth. However, the most effective distortion of my plot is the knowledge of the Holy Spirit. I have warped this truth into a billion different lies, so no one knows what to believe; only a handful of people know that the Holy Spirit has been given to counter and destroy our spiritual activities. So sharp and divisive are the rifts of differences, it produces enemies of the truth, drowning their purpose, daunting their spirits, and minimizing their effect on generations. All I need is a loop hole and I enter, quickly plant my seed, and disappear."

"Generals, you sound so sure of yourselves and your work, but as one who sees into the future and knows what the end will bring, listen so I can instruct you of my ultimate plot; but before we move to this new business, learn from the past.

In the beginning I had a tight grip on the Word. It was held in the hands of only a few, written and spoken only in Latin, and I influenced their minds so carefully they kept it as a personal treasure, hidden from the masses. I want you to be careful of the connected ones. Be on guard for those dedicated to His cause, as it is almost impossible to penetrate their minds. For example, I ordered the execution of Moses at the time of his birth—it was thwarted, with brilliance. Then I coerced him into becoming a violent murderer expecting him to be cast aside, but because of the potent calling on his life, my efforts were blocked. See, he was chosen to write of my humble beginnings. Jeremiah was another: he was persecuted barbarically but still continued to write.

Let me prove to you that persecution does not stop the will of a committed man. John the Baptist reared his head in preparing many for the path of Christ. His love for the wilderness, I believed, would have counted him a lunatic of his time. Instead, many flocked to him for the baptism of repentance. It was necessary to orchestrate his beheading.

Of course, I had been waiting on Jesus to show up. I was stubbornly prepared to fulfill the curse and bruise His heel. He walked into Rome, which was my strong-fort, and through my ingenious craftiness, I surpassed the curse of *bruising His heel*—I shredded His credibility, nullified His miracles, mocked His deity, and finished Him off in crucifixion.

Observing the Great One, I learned a long time ago never to reveal the true intentions of my plans. Therefore, it was not the lack of my craftiness, but unrevealed divine intervention that Jesus showed up at my throne, entering through the gates of death. It floored me, but I am not here to discuss my defeat, I merely wish to show you the progression.

If Jesus did not strip the keys of death and hell from me, we would have had the niche we needed to suffocate the life of man forever. But He stripped me of the dominion I tricked out of Adam.

There is just one caveat that still works in our favor—free will. He left the planet with choice, that now becomes our ammunition. Riddle their guts with the bullets of pleasure that lead to darkness. We must not leave a spark in hell that will not light the fire of doubt and unbelief in their hearts about their God, and we must continue to let them see our fervency as lordship. In their pea-hole of a cranium, they crave the infinite knowledge of Heaven and its glory, not that they might surrender to God, but so they can be puffed up with knowledge and boast against each other. Feed them with ambiguity; take the corruptions of hell and empower them to think it is like unto the power of God. Strengthen their resolve to restlessly increase in destroying each other while labeling it as supernatural power, then brutally entangle them in the chains of condemnation, shame, and guilt until they cannot see the light of forgiveness.

They want an instant active God—they call He is there, they ask, and instantly they receive? Do not let them wait, waiting is doubting. Let them trust you. Listen to their prayers and provide the counterfeit even before God hears them. Be instant in season and out of season. Be watchful, be vigilant, do not waste a moment. Connive, deceive, manipulate, coerce, kill, kill, kill. Kill their spirits, kill their children, use them to kill each other. Breathe hate and intolerance; use genuine love and twist it into betrayal, use their words against them, play with the lack of knowledge of their God, make them honor us as gods. Make them doubt the reality of hell. Give them glamour and glory, they are succors for fame and fortune: they think that pieces of earth that have formed into shiny stones are eternal treasures. Keep them stupid, keep them fighting. We must win.

I diverted from my point, but that Jesus just makes my blood boil, I cannot talk about Him without firing off into a rage. His kingdom must be destroyed and we know how.

Of course, it is my nature to rise up stronger than my fall. I do not see or accept defeat, I learned that from the Great One. Without the keys of my kingdom and my master strategist, death, I could not afford to fold my hands in frustration or walk away in shame. I was unsure of the ultimate plan, but this I realized: if I could rid the planet of the carriers of the Word and the truth, then I could manipulate and mutilate at my leisure, every soul would be mine.

Now to show you how history can serve us: Do not count on any church or organized religion to blindly follow your lead. Know this for certain, wherever the gospel is preached it will eventually lead to the truth. I waited out the shock of the resurrection and the ascension that rattled Jerusalem, then I had to contend with the outpouring of the Holy Spirit at Pentecost, but quietly I began to stir intolerance for the boldness of those whose words ignited the strength of my demise. Slowly I injected the poison of deception into the hearts of those who witnessed with their own eyes Christ's crucifixion. I started with doubt and questions, and as they entertained my thoughts, I spiced my suggestions with the evil of unbelief into every truth they held dear.

I released to the Earth a battalion of venomous demonic warriors to begin a plague of destruction to the work of Christ, and the word on the tongue of every demon in hell was martyrdom. We prophesied it in hell and sang its fear to every heart on Earth. Even those who would not be candidates cowered at the thought of it. Under the rule of the Roman Emperor Nero in 67 AD, the Sanhedrin bribed false witnesses to accuse Stephen of blasphemy against God and Moses. He was the first in a lineup of over two thousand martyrs in Jerusalem, as I poured the fires of hell upon the Church. I marked and timed each one that followed Jesus. James, the brother of Jesus, was beheaded by Herod Agrippa. Philip who converted many in Upper Asia, met with his misfortune of crucifixion when he procured the death of an idolatrous snake-god in Heliopolis. Matthew who wrote his gospel to persuade Jews of the life of Christ, was slain with a halberd in Ethiopia, where he had raised up churches and made many converts.

Mark who traveled with and served as a writer for Peter, was dragged through the streets of Alexandria and left bruised in a dungeon all night before having his body burned the next day. Andrew, the brother of Peter, was tied to his cross with cords to extend the process of suffocation, and no eyes pitied him even though he continued to preach the gospel of Christ while hanging there.

Several attempts were made on Peter. King Agrippa intended to kill him after James was put to death, but he defied magic, escaped from the dungeon of a prison, and more. Finally, after nine months of being chained in prison, he was beaten to a pulp, then crucified, head downwards.

Paul, who was converted at Damascus, I had beheaded; Jude was crucified, Thomas was thrust through with a spear; Luke was hanged. John the Revelator must have had angels inside him. He started the churches in Smyrna, Pergamus, Sardis, Philadelphia, Laodicea, and Thyatira. Emperor Domitian had him thrown into a cauldron of boiling oil, but he walked out of the pot unharmed. Then he was banished to Patmos to work in the mines, yet nothing harmed him. I gave up because I was barred from touching his life.

The barbaric destruction of these twelve men and their disciples lunged the Faith into multiplication faster than I could commit sacrilege. Therefore, I concocted the strategy to destroy from within, pitting one against the other so they persecute each other to death. I also planted seeds of doubt and developed controversy—was Jesus Christ God, or was He man: would Christ have lived on earth in human form: was the Holy Spirit really poured out at Pentecost, or was He still on His way?

These trivial inconsistencies built up such turbulence it divided the Church. Then new writings began. The Apostle's Creed, which outlined the original apostle's beliefs, was written and set in stone to become a holy order. Then came the Cannon, the list of writings some believed were inspired, which eventually became the New Testament. Those who agreed on the same ideas separated themselves from those who did not believe (heretics) and an episcopal governing body was formed. Believers in the Apostle's Creed and the Cannon organized themselves into deacons and presbyters or bishops. The heretics, who followed after my doubts, were the smaller group and they formed churches as well as the canonized group. To distinguish itself, the larger group labeled themselves the Catholic or Universal Church.

The central place of these activities were within the cities, especially Antioch of Syria. Conversion to Christ's doctrine was popular in the city while the country folk remained heathens. I used the country folk or the pagans, to infuse my diabolical plans into church practices.

This inner turbulence created by my ingenious foresight of dividing to conquer was planted in the midst of martyrdom. The followers of Christ or the Christian Church were viewed as weak, ineffective, sacrilegious, and reserved for the poor and indigent. Its core supporters consisted of the uneducated and the socially inept of the time. It had no attractiveness except the steadfast faith of its ardent believers.

On the heels of all this, Emperor Constantine secured a tremendous victory over his rival Maxentius to conquer Rome. He attributed his triumph to his vision of the cross over the sun and words of inspiration at a critical time when many thought he would have lost the battle. He was a faithful servant of mine, serving the Persian sun-god, Mithra, but after the vision and victory, he converted to Christianity and elevated the religion and its teachings to be equal to the laws of the Roman Empire. This insult to us, generals, cannot be overstated. It was as though the blood of the martyrs were hurled into our teeth, and mocked us with a venom that ruptured the caverns of hell.

In his reign as emperor of Rome, Constantine sewed together the many churches that were hidden in caves and underground hideouts, poured wealth and stature into their treasury, built new churches, established Sunday as the principal day of worship and the day of rest, but most of all, he brought the bishops together to a council in Nicea of Asia Minor to end their controversy and bitterness and establish order concerning that which divided them.

The Nicene Creed was written as the foundation of the Canonized Church, that Jesus Christ is the very God, begotten, not created, and having the very essence or being as the Father God. The foundational orthodox of historical Christian truth was now laid on the table, and out of that council of bishops, a father, a *papas*, a Papa, was chosen to lead them, and the Pope was born.

Again, I seized the opportunity to contaminate from within. I twisted the celebrations of Passover with the worship of the sun god and the solar calendar and labeled it Easter, then allowed the emperor to enjoy his reign as long as he continued to muddle the heart of the truth with my slime of pagan worship.

Immediately after Saint Constantine died, I reverted to martyrdom. Emperor Trajan gave orders to exterminate the stock of David, threw the Bishop of Pontus into a hot-lime kiln then removed him and threw him into a scalding bath until he died. He placed fire in the hands of the Bishop of Antioch while papers dipped in oil were placed at his side and set ablaze. After this light torture, he was dispatched to be torn to pieces by wild beasts. We had men fastened to posts, then drawn by pulleys to dislocate their limbs because they refused to make sacrifices to our heathen gods.

In the reign of Antonius Pius, the horrors of persecution increased. Martyrs had to walk with wounded feet over thorns, nails, and other sharp objects. Christians were scourged until their flesh and veins lay bare. Polycarpus, the Bishop of Smyrna, a disciple of John the Revelator, at eighty-seven years old, was set ablaze at the stake, but his praises to God rendered his body unconsumed. The guards, determined to put an end to him, drove spears into his body, but the quantity of blood that pulsed from the wounds quenched the vehemently hot flames. After considerable attempts, they put him to death, then burned the dead body, not being able to burn it while he was alive.

Again, I caution you, it is impossible to wipe out the church with persecution. Persecution builds character and strengthens the resolve of its witnesses. The purpose of our meeting today is to point out that the only strategy that has not yet been employed is the complete removal of the Bible from the hands and the hearts of man. The anointing of that book makes me fear and tremble because those who drink its words walk out of darkness into the arms of His love.

The truth went wild when John Wycliffe, advocating the benefit of The Book's knowledge to the common people, rebelled against the Pope's order and translated the Bible from Latin into English. Martin Luther reproduced the translation into German and went on to denounce the activities of the Canonized Church with his 95 Thesis of Contention, a writing which pointed out the crimes that had begun to infect the Catholic Church in Rome. These crimes were the lies I had subtly inserted into the Church through Constantine and the pagans to contaminate the truth.

However, shortly after these translations, children learned to pray. Do not allow the children in your grasp to pray. If you do, they will forever trust in God. Something about their tender souls crying out to God seals them to Him for eternity. Children that do not learn to pray are easy targets—they trust us.

I underestimated Johann Gutenberg when he began toying with the idea of inventing a printing press. He transformed the invention into a Bible printery. I quickly fixed that with unscrupulous sorts who stole his invention and left him penniless. Next came Thomas Linacre, he is the prime example of why we should take education from children born into the knowledge of God. Once he learned Greek, he compared his translated Bible to the original Latin Vulgate version and there began the correction of errors given in the translations.

Even through the plight of execution, John Colet, son of the mayor of London in 1496, persevered and translated an English version of the Bible and taught it in Saint Paul's Cathedral. Erasmus used original manuscripts to make the corrections Colet discovered. Tyndale, who mastered eight languages, worked with Martin Luther and completed the printing of the New Testament to the English language.

It became necessary to wipe out these projects. I chased Tyndale out of England to sabotage his writing. The entire nation came under pressure to burn the books or risk death. He was relentless but it was not long before he was burned at the stake. Myles Coverdale and Thomas Matthew, disciples of Tyndale, were the ones to combine Old and New Testaments for printing in as far back as 1535. King Henry VIII had steadfastly resisted the printing and distribution of The Book, but his falling out with the Roman Catholic Pope, led Henry to rebel by publishing the Great Bible, then fund and print legal English copies.

I could go on to tell you about the Geneva Convention and the printing of the Geneva Bible, which I have securely removed out of print. It had the format and accuracy I did not want in circulation. King James came along in the 1600s and began chaining his edition of the Bible to pulpits in England. His original version contained the Apocrypha, which mixed magic with the Word. The Protestants removed the books of the Apocrypha from his version in the late 1800s which eventually led to the widespread of denominations and religious fanatics.

These historical facts must serve to increase our strategy. Persecution of true believers promotes the Word. Starve men of the presence of God and they run to seek Him. Hide the truth and men become hunters of God. However, let me lay out our new strategy.

Knowledge has increased. The days of Gutenberg's printing are over. At the push of a button, billions of Bibles are produced and distributed digitally. We know better than to prohibit distribution now. However, we will quickly move into an era where everything is digitally produced. Before you get excited, listen carefully. We must desensitize man to this new commodity. His food, his clothes, and his life must be shelved around technology and a virtual software network. Desensitize their privacy and get them familiar with meeting pictorially. Relationships, business transactions, new inventions—all must revolve around this technological virtual cloud we are building. Familiarize man with the notion that his information can be safely stored in this virtual network and retrieved at the push of a button. One failure or glitch in the system will set us back years, so plan explicitly. As they trust in the convenience of my technologically advanced virtual reality, we outdate and destroy the use of traditional printing and communication. Live communication then will become the irresistible wave, enhanced by graphic designs, breathing in color, with full animation.

Then it will come to pass; first, we will contaminate The Book by removing truth and sowing lies into key chapters and verses. We will give that era some time to breathe so the pollution and lies can populate and take root in the heart of man. Ultimately, when they go back to searching out the truth, we control the knowledge and the plug. The ultimate goal will be to use the reigning authority, the antichrist, to pull The Book and all other evidence of the knowledge of God completely out of circulation, soak our own bible into the slime of deceit, insert our own religious rites and doctrines, and feed them our truth straight into hell— the way to the spiritual unknown.

My efforts to wipe the truth from the hearts of mankind failed in the past only because the Bible, which contains potent understanding of truth sanctioned by the Great One, was not destroyed. The second great plot will be to manipulate our own virtual cloud to ransom and harvest even more fools. Once we control the virtual technological cloud, we will extract their souls to tap into their own information. That will be the ultimate control. We will link their collected data to a monopoly and sell, sell, sell—at the price of blood.

I will be honored through time and eternity as the only prince who had the balls to overthrow God's kingdom and steal the greatest gift and treasure of His heart, His precious children. That honor can no one take away. Let's not back down or melt away. We are greater than man, we must defeat them. Do not allow them...

"Commander, Master, help! There is ma-massive bloodshed, we arrrr defeat-te-tu-hed. Men-men, many wo-wound, lifeless, huh-huh, Commander, Co-co-man." The ghoul could not continue his pleas; he had been skinned to a bloody mess, like an animal shaved by a butcher, lifeless and out of breath he sank to the floor.

The commander's aide rushed across the room and began rolling the gigantic ball that was suspended in mid-air. One by one, the generals began to stand and head towards the globe to see the trouble which had interrupted the meeting. The master of the ghoul who had brought the bad news glanced over at his close comrade. No one cared to help him, and he would not dare disrupt the flow of order. The commander had identified the trouble and was giving instructions, he knew better than to show sympathy.

"—mismanaged control. I need troops from the Northwest, and the Southern tip, they are familiar with this kind of war. This has the glow of fervent prayer. This was a covert job. I need four generals on this job, stationed at the four winds. The winds will alert you as to what is coming. Your task is to watch and to pour strength into the fighters. I need two powers to roll in from beneath; there must be an open entry way: a tunnel, a cave, an underground joint, or a filthy church basement, one of those that we have used as a cemetery for our priestly abortions. Roll in and find a good human shield to enter, then go snooping to find the source of the prayer. Once you find it, do not try to be a hero, send a report to the general at the East Wind and wait for instructions.

Next, I see only two strong angelic warriors stationed to fight; see, one at the cathedral and another covering that home, the other angels are fighters, so gather our fighters from everywhere to go in. However, I do not want this reinforcement to fight, I want them to go in as angels of light. If the prayers are not strong they will not be detected. Go in, lay low, and observe. Fighters, communicate your findings to the East Wind general, the general will send word to my principal. I will disseminate word on the attack. Go!

Generals, one crucial factor still exists, there is far too much fighting in our ranks. Division destroys the best laid plans. Who knows better than you that the deadliest force to destroy a sure-proof plan is division. If you continue to tear and devour each other, we will have no souls to torment in the hereafter. If only for your own sakes, get along.

Now go!"

CHAPTER 10

Shatter the Hold

It was indeed a long day at work, enjoyable, but certainly mysterious, and long. She couldn't get him off her mind, and it wasn't the broken bones or the bacterial pneumonia stemming from the severe malnourishment and improper care at the prison, nor was it the miracle of him coming out of the coma: there was something more. She would take it to the secret place with her Lord and find out.

It was early evening, and Martha's car was parked in its usual spot. A few other cars she could not identify were there, but it was not crowded, so she could escape unidentified. She opened the door and slipped into the sanctuary intending to go to the prayer room, but as she passed by the altar she felt compelled to kneel before the replica of the Ark of the Covenant.

As she knelt she felt covered in the presence of the Almighty God. Oh the sense of His glorious presence: the peace, the joy, the heart of worship. Tears welled up in her eyes, and a hymn poured out from her lips.

"Draw me nearer, nearer, nearer blessed Lord to the cross where Thou hast died. Draw me nearer, nearer,

nearer blessed Lord, to Thy precious bleeding side." Her lips mumbled the tune as the words became mixed with her gentle sobs of reverence.

"Dear Lord, I prostrate myself at Your feet, humbled to be in Your presence, delighted to be a chosen vessel for Your glory. I enter into the Holy of Holies, by faith, by the blood of Your Son the Lord Jesus Christ. You are my Lord and I worship You. You alone are holy; holy and righteous, glorious and wonderful."

The gentle weeping was mixed with the muffled sounds of praise as she closed her eyes allowing her tears to speak its language of gratitude and adoration to her Father God.

Her thoughts drifted to the replica at which she kneeled. This was the place where God promised to visit His people. She smiled. "Are You here, Lord? Have You sent Your Holy Spirit?" Her heart welled up again, and her eyes began to overflow. She bowed her head to her knees and allowed the presence of the Lord to overwhelm her. "I love You, Lord, my God, with all my heart, I love You. Thank You for visiting me, thank You for loving me, thank You for Your sweet presence.

Again her thoughts drifted to the replica, there were the angels just above the mercy seat... the mercy seat, the mercy seat. The words kept ringing in her mind. "Are You asking me to cry out to You that Your mercy may be poured out, Father? Lord, I beseech Your throne for Your mercy to be poured out. Pour out Your mercy on me, on David, on this Church. Father, pour out Your mercy on this town. Heavenly Father, there are people right now that are in danger of reaping the wages of sin, but I pray for Your mercy. Release Your angels to fight for Your chosen; release Your angels with strength and might to do battle on behalf of Your people. You said that If Your people who are called by Your name will humble themselves and pray, and seek Your face, and turn from their wicked ways; then You will hear from Heaven and forgive their sins and heal their land. Heal this land, Lord, heal our hearts from its stubbornness; rid us of deceit and lies and the pride that keeps us out of Your presence. Father, You know when we have believed a lie, You know where the enemy has laid his carefully plotted tracks that keep us bound to darkness; so Father, I cry out on behalf of Your people, Your people who have been yoked to the slavery of sin and chained by the blackmail of shame; I cry out on behalf of Your children who have been sold and bought by the lies of hell. Father, redeem, through the blood of Jesus Christ Your Son, make that eternal purchase now. Deliver from the realms of darkness, from the shadow of death, the souls tormented by evil. Release a cry from the lips of the souls You have kept as the apple of Your eye. Release the word, Jesus; release the word, mercy; release the word, help; and redeem them from the strongholds of hell.

In the name of Jesus Christ our Savior, I bind the forces of darkness. I bind principalities and powers, the rulers of darkness, dominion, might, spiritual wickedness in high places, and every thought that has exalted itself against the knowledge of God I cast down in the Name of Jesus Christ. I ask for the pure blood of Christ to be poured out now on the souls for which our Savior is interceding; let the redeeming power of the blood of Christ free them from the yoke and the strongholds of the forces of hell."

A strong and familiar hand glided across her waist. The shock of the touch made her flinch; it was intimate, it was personal, it was David. "Honey, you scared me!" Her soft voice was shaky as she reached out and hugged his neck, laying her head on his hard chest.

"I know, I'm sorry." He kissed her head. "I was at home and I could feel your prayers. Somehow I knew you were here, and I came searching for you."

She could hear his heart pounding inside his chest. Her heart was smiling as he held her gently. "As I came into the sanctuary, I could hear the voice of God walking up and down these aisles. Your prayers are so powerful, I could see them reaching up over the church and into the air like beams going forth over the land, like waves, bringing life and healing."

She looked into his eyes and saw the soul of the man she had married seventeen years ago. He was a man that loved God and walked before Him in integrity, a man who had given up his dream of being a corporate guru to study the laws and teachings of the Almighty God, and she loved him. Yes, for a moment in time, however long that was, he had diverted, but now, now her husband was by her side interceding for his people.

"Look around you!"

She raised her head. The sanctuary was almost full. People were kneeling, others were standing, but all were praying. "I called a few people, and Martha called a few Churches. It is time to pray. Come on, let's stand."

"Saints, please give me a moment of your time." He waited a few seconds as they gathered to the center of the room. "We initiated this meeting because my wife and I have sensed a spiritual urgency to mount up a defense of prayer for this town and its surroundings, all the way into the city. I know in your heart you have heard the urgency of this petition and that you are ready to pray. However, before we proceed to the matter at hand, I want to lay the foundation of prayer, so please be seated for a few moments.

There are truths we must consider and implement in order to become effective in our warfare of prayer. Every soldier going to war must be trained in combat with specific knowledge on how to engage his weapons to destroy his enemy. Ephesians tells us that we wrestle not against flesh and blood but against principalities and powers, against the rulers of the darkness of this world, against spiritual wickedness in high places. Since we possess this knowledge, we must take the whole armor of God that in the evil day we would not fall.

Two other Scriptures to bear in mind: if a man is a sinner, God does not hear him, and, they that worship God must worship Him in Spirit and in truth. When Jesus rose from the dead, He appeared to His disciples and proved to them that He was indeed the Christ by showing them the prints of the nails in His hands and feet. To dispel their doubts He said to them, 'a ghost does not have flesh and bones.' Then Jesus gave them a glimpse of the afterlife, the life we will inherit with our Father God when we die: Jesus took fish and honeycomb and ate with them.

From this we conclude that the immortal body will have flesh and bones, with the purified blood from our Father God that will not be able to be contaminated with sin. Sin contaminated God's creation and today we are battling with the forces of darkness whose sole existence is to destroy the beauty God designed for the Earth. How then will the purity of God be maintained when He sovereignly puts an end to the rule of evil?

The answer is worship. As immortal beings we will be able to eat and drink and enjoy the pleasures we do here on Earth with the exception of marriage. Why? The purpose of marriage is to form the intimate bonding exchange of worship, where the two become one. This pinnacle of worship unites the heart, soul, mind, and body and becomes the ultimate picture of selfless giving and abandonment while releasing the core of our innermost parts to mingle in the ultimate pleasure of intimacy. Worship then can only be embodied with one. We do not have the capacity to share our being in bonding intimacy with more than one individual at a time. Therefore, the Lord says to Israel, I am one God, a jealous God, and you shall worship no other god. Reserve your intimacy, your worship for me alone and let us become one. The ultimate intimate bonding, where two become one—that is worship.

In Matthew chapter 22 and verse 30, Jesus supplied the answer of God's design to keep the new Heaven and the new Earth pure; He removed the possibility of contamination by removing the capacity to bond and ultimately become one with any but God alone.

Again, they that worship God must worship Him in Spirit and in truth. Worshiping in spirit therefore is the bonding unity of intimacy with the only true God and a glimpse of that intimacy is felt when our hearts are bonded in marriage to one. As we try desperately to understand this bond of worship, we can see marriage producing offsprings—two becoming one. Further, bonding spiritually in marriage brings joy and happiness; but break that bond by introducing another or many others, and our hearts are ripped and torn, producing evil, producing the worship of many gods.

Sin, taking occasion by the flesh, deceived us into corrupting this bonding intimacy with one, as it was designed, into wildly propagating this worship to many. Sarai, who could bare no children, displaced herself when she gave her Egyptian maid to her husband so she could enjoy the pleasure of having a son. That inconceivable act of achieving the desire of the flesh and mind has yielded an unending merciless bloodshed between the two brothers as long as we have known them.

Infecting the worship of one by bonding with many, corrupts worship in many ways: the mind is infected, the heart produces evil, and the body is weakened by sickness. First, the mind has to be coerced or lured into polluting and devaluing that which was virtuous and sacred by the poisonous thoughts of selfish enjoyment and egotistical fulfillment. By entertaining this deceit, we surrender to the spirit of perverted worship—which is the spirit of serving many gods. The spirit of polytheism despises the spirit of unity.

The worship of many gods produces hearts that are filled with impurity, filled with thoughts of how to conjure lies which benefit selfishness in order to fulfill sensual pleasures—the heart then cannot be true, cannot be pure, and cannot produce joy or love. In this corrupted exchange of intimacy, each person gives themselves on the notion of a gamble or for the selfish desires of pleasure. Without the purity of a true heart, it is impossible for man to trust or serve his brother or God, because his heart is divided. His divided heart then begins to devise evil against that which he mistrusts, and that theory just keeps expanding.

Many ask the question today, where is God when evil so blatantly overruns the earth? If there is a God, why, why, why? Yet they ignorantly perpetrate the very evil they question. Only the carriers of evil question God's existence. Only those who are blinded to truth seek after another god except the true and living God who sent His Son Jesus Christ to be our Lord and Savior. If we truly examine our lives and become accountable to our actions, we would find that our love and purity has been so stained with the filth and the greed of grabbing after idols and their promise of earthly offerings, that we have lost, and I do mean *lost* the sense of humility to even believe, never mind trust in the purity of the one true God.

Just as it is spiritually, so it is in the body; we reap the effects of the mixing of several different body fluids when we give ourselves to many partners. Different bodily fluids commingle in our blood and conflict with each other; each fighting for its place to be at peace, and finding no rest, the immune system of our body, in a tumultuous roller coaster, begins to reject and spit the combination of various partners out of the system as disease. Simply, the body cannot drink pleasurably in intimacy from many fountains, it will become diseased and die.

The emotional tumult solicits the spirit of divorce, which is the tearing apart, the separating of intimate worship, of the one chosen and consecrated by God for worship. Imagine the breach of a pregnancy in a mother's womb. The womb is the safe haven to conceive and nurture a new birth until it is able to be placed on the pedestal of the Earth and bring joy to the mother and father who conceived it in intimate worship. A breach in this nurturing environment is a rip, a tear, a rupture that introduces unwanted elements into the process of nurturing, then putrefaction and decay produces a stench likely to ooze from the very pores of the mother. Without intervention, both the nurturer and the nurtured will die. Divorce is a breach in the covenant of worship with one. God says, 'I hate divorce.' In Proverbs chapter 30 and verse 20, the adulterous woman eats then wipes her mouth and says, 'I have done no wickedness.' Jesus referred to the Scribes and Pharisees in Matthew 12 as an adulterous and evil generation who wanted a sign to prove His deity, because if they could prove His deity they would worship Him. He referred them to the sign of Jonah, who preached and the people believed and repented. In order for us to return from the evil of perverted worship we must trust the sign of the spoken and the written word of Jehovah God and repent.

Repentance is the turning away from the gods of our understanding and the yielding of our beings in total abandonment to our Creator God. This state of abandonment is not a careless or reckless giving over of the will and desires, but rather the willing submission of the strength and might we possess, the surrender of the determination and fervor to accomplish the undying passion of our souls; this will is purposely handed over to our sovereign God, Jehovah, through

His Son the Lord Jesus Christ, and in turn, we seek His face to hear His heart for our lives. Why? Because His knowledge and wisdom so infinitely surpasses that which we can ask or imagine.

Now, they that come to God, He will in no way cast them out—that is God's promise. Therefore, forgiveness of sins is ours to enjoy. As we stand before a holy God, with full understanding of His word and His will, we bow our hearts in prayer that we may become His voice spoken in the earth. How do we know what we ought to pray? First, we enter into the gates of prayer with thanksgiving, speaking out our adoration for His Majesty, expressing gratitude with honor and praise. It is in this genuine expression of verbal worship that we are ushered by the Holy Spirit to the throne of His Majesty. We know we have entered the throne room when we become immersed in His glory and our words are transformed to speaking, not from our understanding or our desires, but from His heart, the heart of God. When we speak from His heart we intercede on a spiritual level, and the voice of God is released in the Earth accomplishing God's divine purpose. Our vision becomes enlightened and as we build this intimate exchange with God, we begin to know His heart, His desire. It is a spiritual encounter, a gift that flows as His words come alive in our souls and our desires, and God manifests Himself to us deep within the recesses of our being, as man becomes one with the Almighty God. The purpose of this vision, of this spiritual encounter is, 'Thy kingdom come, Thy will be done,' because without this vision we perish.

Mary, the mother of Jesus, experienced the vision when she encountered the angel and said, 'be it unto me according to Your words:' David caught the vision when he prophesied to Goliath, 'I will take your head from you today and give your flesh to the dogs:' Joshua saw the vision when he drew his sword to slay the angel. Angels carry out the will of God in the heavenly realms, and man carries out the will of God in the Earth. Without this vision we perish; we die slowly while blaming everyone around us for the trouble we see.

Let me encourage you to enter into the Holy Place before the Most High God and pledge to Him alone your intimate spiritual worship. Do not allow God to be discredited because you failed; give God no rest until He makes this town, this city His praise in the Earth. You are my witnesses, says the Lord, that I am God; you are my witness that I heal, then speak forth my healing to those who are sick: you are my witnesses that I supply needs, then distribute my provision to those in need: you are my witnesses that I am love, then let your voice bring healing and your hands be extended in love.

The words of the prophet Amos that he saw. Yes, he saw the words come to life. "In the last days, says the Lord, I will pour out my spirit on all flesh." God desires to pour His Spirit on flesh. Are you a candidate for His spirit? Are you flesh? Then let God pour His Spirit on flesh. Speak to Him now, say, "Lord I am flesh, pour out Your Spirit on me."

Move beyond that which weighs you down and capture the vision of the Holy Spirit; Christ fulfilled His ministry in the midst of adversity. Do not wish your adversity away. Instead, demolish the turmoil through steadfast obedience to God's direction, destroy the path of evil by paving a path of purity in worship, build your intimacy with the Holy Lamb of God, and begin to utter His prophetic voice in this city. Let the quickening anointing that is poured out upon flesh and the holy covenant given to you through the blood of Jesus Christ our Lord sanctify your hearts and minds and pull you into the unity of the Spirit so that the divine will of God for this city may be established.

Let us pray."

CHAPTER 11

The Gig Is Up, Way Up

"Commander, the town is indeed fortified, but we have identified significant loopholes, which, with careful manipulation, will be our gateway of entry and means of takeover. May I address the orders and present my strategy for the operation?"

The commander nodded his approval, his beady eyes glaring under the scorn of the torture that had ruptured a prime territory.

"Principals and orders, let me advise you as to the severity of this matter. We have detected the discipline of fervent prayer. Not only has it been fervent, but there has been a steadfast adherence to her promise that has not been compromised. Yes, it is the work of one woman. She has borne in her body the scars of rejection and humiliation; the scorn of infidelity, the grief of losing her father who was dear to her heart, and physical prints that would be far too much to tell: yet she has single-handedly mounted the armed defense of the angelic hosts for her town and all the other towns leading up to the city limits, without flinching.

Her fervency has also attracted a steady following of prayer warriors. This body of intercessors was birthed through her supplication to the Almighty and are strategically staged throughout the towns. Some of them know each other physically, but not all, even though they pray in unison. Needless to say, these homes are forts that sport strong beacons of light and attract legions of angels that transport messages back and forth to the beyond. As we speak, the territory has been reinforced with warrior angels who are on guard; two generals have been identified, which tells us the territory is deemed important.

What do we have and where does our strength lie? We have a ghetto project, an outlier of the town that is minimally controlled. It is run by the spirit of Poverty, but there has not been much dirt in it. There are no gangs, no rape, no violent spirits hanging around. We snooped around and the only spirit we found with any influence was Gambling, and it did not carry a ring with it. We found the churchy-type grandparents caring for grandchildren and we have designed a plot to penetrate that.

We snooped around Town Hall and found a controlled sect who prided themselves as affiliates of the largest church in town and others who could not care less. We could use Sabotage there.

A low level of gambling was spotted at various places, but everything was religiously controlled. Control did exert a strong presence, and even though he is gone, the habitual practice of obedience to the spirit is overly strong.

Therefore, we do not have enough ground to stand on in that town, however, our ammunition lies in the surrounding towns. Just outside the town, westward, heading toward the city, is one of our churches. It is the huge stonework edifice that sits on nine acres of land. The entrance was designed with a glorified brass and wooden door beneath overshadowing stone art that simulates the entry into a tomb. There we have massacred the lives of countless unborn babies and laid them to rest in its basement. Various chambers, halls, and vaults have been dedicated to us, plus we are treated with the respect and dignity we deserve at this rest site. It will be our base. As of yet, it is not considered a threat, and because it is outside the immediate war zone, we should be safe.

Here are the plans. The first phase of our strategy is to empower and arm our ground fighter team for the take-over. At six o'clock on Friday evening, we will blow up the tunnel taking rush-hour traffic out of the city; that will be our first feat. On Saturday morning we will highjack and overturn the five o'clock train going into the city. These will provide enough ammunition for all the foot workers. Two generals are assigned to these specific tasks, and they have already assembled their demolition teams. Everyone is invited to glean from these two enterprises.

These massacres will set the stage for despair, throwing even the most diligent off guard, and at that point, we will converge on the towns and identify random victims as individual sacrifices to further strengthen our position for this operation.

From there, we will ride up the coast through the various towns in the direction of our main target. Loversville is a great peddling point for random looting, rape, breaking and entering, you name it.

Do not be afraid to stage accidents, gun violence, drug overdoses, and heart attacks; and even if the victim is not dead on the first attack, wrap yourself around them like an angel of light and entice them into giving up their lives so you can finish off each job. This phase will be most effective through the weekend.

Our goal is to drive up the level of fear and encourage negative talk to drown out the effect of prayer. We must stir up diabolical fear and terror in their hearts and have them speak doom and destruction out of hearts of fear. If we can mount these words of death into a substantial structure, we can weaken the effect of prayer over the region. The weakening of prayers has already begun as those who are stationed undercover have been surfacing at nights when the righteous are asleep, entering into dreams and keeping awake through nightmares those through whom we gain permission to enter.

Sunday morning will begin our second phase. Everyone must be gathered at the base by dawn on Sunday morning. Please gather in the basement. Too many of us roaming around in the sanctuary would throw the morning worshipers into chaos, so please be respectful. I believe our commander will be in attendance and will be honored at the morning service, so again, please be respectful.

At the base we will be briefed on the state of affairs of the town. At that point we should have wreaked enough havoc in the surrounding towns and the city to see a change in the guards over the town. Needless to say, our target is David and Angelique. We know we cannot come near or touch Angelique, but David has been a puppet for so long, all we need to do is to isolate him from Angelique to take him out. This is where you can become a hero. Our commander is offering a double promotion in rank to the soldier who assassinates David and burns the church.

We will not waste time. Immediately after our briefing we will begin the looting and the violence. It will be a spillover of Saturday night's rage into Sunday. Our major strategy is to burn down buildings and destroy the fabric of the town. By sundown, the town should be on fire. We have lots of people we can transport from the city into the town to assist in the massacre, and they are not valuable, it won't matter if we lose them. Once we have gained momentum from those incidents, we are ready for David and Angelique. That should be fun."

"General," the commander raised his hand to silence the general, "I will not leave the task of destroying this target to anyone. I will undertake it myself. I have watched her every move since this matter was brought to my attention. She is indeed a jewel of purity. She has set guards over her heart, over her words, and over her senses, but she has one flaw. Her weakness is the need for her father's devotion. As a child, she was nurtured and beloved by her father; his passing has left a vacuum that weakens her heart. She has been yearning to have David fill the role. If I take David, she will fall apart; her prayers will cease and then I will transform my layers and plague her with depression. I will lead her to blame herself for David's death and melt the strength of her prayer, then convince her that her place is with David. If I can't have her, I will encourage her to take a premature visit to her maker.

General, I noted that you did not address the cue that generated the fortifying of the town. What propelled Angelique into becoming a spiritual general? Demand gives rise to supply. Therefore, as long as those conditions exist, our problems will resurface with invigorated and unmatched strength."

"Commander, it was her father—he laid a solid foundation of love and trust for, for, ahhh, for, well. He taught her the secrets of prayer, taught her to secure covenants with the Most High by completing her God-given assignments, then how to humble herself and offer her body as a living sacrifice to Him. He taught her the honor of purity to enter the throne room of her Lord, and the virtue poured out in worship. She walks into the Holy Place of the Spirit as if it were an early tabernacle, and she has secured a place in His heart. She is dear and precious to Him."

"Yes, yes, that is all true, but a special relationship does not warrant the kind of coverage she provided for the town and the towns around her. She fortified an entire region and threw hemorrhage in the realms of darkness, bringing deliverance to countless souls, even souls she has never met. She retrieved inside knowledge from the Holy Spirit and stole Adia's sacrifice."

The room burst out in mumbles of shock. It took more than a minute to quiet the rumbles as each beast began to recount the unexplainable defeat it had encountered.

"I demand silence." He waited a moment as all eyes turned to him. "Your ignorance has cost us an entire region. I have released orders to bring Adia here on this side. She has to pay for her careless flaunting and inability to secure our territory. She hesitated to provide sacrificial offerings over and over again, preferring to protect her image over obedience. Instead, her waves of activity disturbed the region, stirring up the need for combative prayer. Angelique detected the supernatural stronghold of the occult, and by utilizing the Passover Cup, she covenanted with her Lord to erase the legal holds of past blood sacrifices and prevent future dedications. Her prayers have been more than effective—we have lost monumentally.

The plan to stage multiple accidental deaths for this territory will help us to gain ground. I will not tolerate failure or treachery in this operation. We need the blood of martyrdom to counter the blood of the Passover Cup that has secured the region. Take note of the faces you are about to see, we have secured these targets as our means of restoring our debauchery in the region. I will be watching this operation with keen eyes." He walked out.

The room broke out into mumbles again. The general conducting the meeting was floored. He did not realize the magnitude of the failure. Adia was his, but no one told him she was ordered for chains. He was upstaged and his pride had his dedication to this operation fumbled. What deceit, what a backstabbing, conniving brood of devils? Hell never failed to surprise him. The higher he rose in the ranks, the greater the unfaithfulness, the greater the hate and the rivalry. He was done: he would sabotage the operation and save Adia.

His principal observed his confusion and rose to finish the orders for the operation. He turned and whiffed out in a puff of smoke.

"In phase three of the operation, we will focus on plaguing and possessing specific individuals. Please take note of the faces that are now brought into focus. Principals and orders will carry out this operation, so watch carefully: these are your targets.

This is the mayor of Londonsville and a major supporter of David's church. He is the glue to the business moguls that attend the church. He is a glutton and proud of it. We have placed commodities at his fingertips that will lead this unsuspecting baboon to a lifeless corpse. As he craves new flavors, quick fixes, and instant gratification, we have spiced his sustenance with sugars, and cholesterols, and salts for that irresistible taste, while hidden in its core are chemicals which will slowly lead this threat to his final resting place.

This grandmother lives on Ticket Lane. She has been a faithful church goer all her life, and has not been acquainted with worldly ideas or the changing times—by that I mean she is a trusting soul. Angelique trusts her to stand by her side in prayer for difficult matters. This boy is her grandson, she knows of him, met him a couple of times, loves and prays for him diligently. He is a gang member turned snitch and about to be sacrificed by the gang. We are bringing him to the grandmother where he thinks he will be safe, and he will be accompanied by a host of demons which we will unload into the house to break the woman's faith; then we will bring the gang there to take both of them. Just for keeps, we will have the gang hang out at the house for a while to survey the possibility of staying in town.

This man is David's best friend and special advisor for the growth of the church. He runs the largest brokerage house, covering most of the territory. He is extremely busy and extremely valuable to us. His foolish heart has been burdened to supply his family with more and more possessions, while he misses out on their relationships and tenderness and the joy of just living. Further, we have inserted the trap of misunderstanding and hurriedness into the sample, so the values and goodwill that remain will become stained with unpleasantries. It used to be that the opposite of love is hate, but his family's notion of love has become *show me the money*. With that, we have added the burden to live beyond their capacity to attain, and the home has been strained to bursting point. He is ready for a heart attack, let it become a reality, quickly.

This woman is a teacher who looks to the church for her standards to influence the high school of the town. She is an old-fashion doofus who carves out an atmosphere of wholesomeness and truth, advocating that children live as if the Lord God were walking and talking with them as a friend. Instead of her, we need an avid believer in technology because ninety-nine percent of our computer games are loaded with death or cheating, and some are just outright witchcraft. We have not overlooked any area. We want girls to play with our spirits, which we have decorated and called fairies; no one has connected the dots that anything other than birds or insects that fly, especially imaginary flying beings, must be spiritual. Through these toys which they have come to love and cherish, we are able to get into their dreams and influence their thoughts. In their nightmares, we will portray them as deserving of punishment, make them see themselves as evil, and then continue to infiltrate them with behaviors that boggle the minds of adults.

This is the police chief of the city, but he has influence in every town we need to take over. He is ruthless in his tactics but righteous in his rule. We need to celebrate his funeral. Why? Corruption in law enforcement breeds violence. Corruption is the fuel we use to stoke the fire of trouble, and when it bleeds into the turf, all we need to do is strike a match. One of our most potent match is to plant a gun in the hand of every male under the age of fifty and riddle them with an overpowering sense and urgency to use it.

You heard me correctly: when boys handle guns as early as they can make a fist, the toys place the feel of the power of the weapon in their hand and the word kill on their tongue. In order to build on the momentum, we portray death in their entertainment, then desensitize them to the reality by placing it daily on the news. Over and over again, as they enjoy the simulated games they are forced to kill, and then announce, *he's dead*. The games help to remove the reality of the destructiveness of death from their consciousness, and so many cannot wait to use a real gun. These ideas planted in their minds grow like a well-watered garden. They don't even question the source of their ideas, they just drink from our fountain of lies, freely.

This plot has been so effective in other regions we do not have to influence the use of the gun, and because they practiced on their brothers using the toys, they use the real weapon on their brothers as well. When we have a body, we visit them with the blame game. Everyone that fires a fatal shot has the ultimate blame for someone else, because none of them see the gun as death; they foolishly see it as protection. We must get rid of righteous rule.

Next, we have no slime, no filth, no nauseating joints that celebrate hell in the town. Therefore, this man is our candidate to start a chain of strip bars and night clubs with finances from his drug ring. He will be set up to buy the burnt-out church and start his best operation there. For those of you who do not understand the power of the nightclub, please allow me to explain."

A gush of wind swept through the room overturning everything in its wake, then doubled back creating a mini quake and upsetting the spiritual room. It was the commander, his fury smelled like burning coals of sulphur.

"Treason, I detect treason. Where is it?" He looked around ready to shred to pieces anyone who dared to move. "Norion, where is he, where is he?"

"Sick, sick, vomiting sick, needed a moment. I... I, I filled in for smooth operation, this is my best." His muffled words were just above a whisper.

As the commander's odor simmered, he adjusted his boldness to gain favor.

"I was just about to show how we can commemorate your glory in the Earth. With your permission, Your Highness, I will continue." The silence was loud. It seemed as if he bought the lie that Norion was sick.

"Commander, we have so many songs that commemorate your achievements in the earth, so many songs that glorify and give you credit. Our chants and rhymes have made it into the vernacular of countless generations. They are ignorant of the truth that their words are assignments which are carried out spiritually, so we twist their minds into singing these words of defeat underlined with subtle death, which feeds us with the fire we need to carry out our evil desires. The nightclub is an ingenious design for the promotion of our songs, and as they dance to them, we dance our way into their souls; as they sing the words, we bring them alive in their lives.

We feed men the unsatisfying desire of lust, lust so strong it cannot be satisfied by the normal use of a woman. The fire inside leads them to search out men, children, and even animals. As they feed these cravings we are transferred from body to body, and the trail of evil is untold.

In these clubs we reduce girls to the label of a wanton female dog. Commander, none of this is coincidental and we thrive on it. As soon as they accept the label, we assign them the spiritual counterpart that takes the words and makes them a reality. We have produced the highest order of whoredom, prostitution, and abortions out of these lusting strategies with the nightclub as our church."

The word abortion lightened the commander and set him at ease, and he gave the principal a nonverbal grin of approval.

"Commander, once the stage is set and all these plans have been implemented we will erect a Department of Deception at the base on the border of the town, and true to our nature, we will stealthily penetrate the territory. Our map and sphere of influence will be like that of the spider—in the king's palace yet found in the tattered coat of the homeless. We will infiltrate weddings for the sole reason of corrupting the perfect picture of the family; we will be at funerals comforting the rejectors of truth when the dead is trapped in a Christless eternity. We will hoist our flags on many cathedrals as we ruin the truth of His Word with the inner core of our nature. We will carve out injustice and intolerance as a sword in the political arena at the price of gold. We will lean heavily on the ignorant and the unlearned, and for those who seek knowledge and wealth for their selfish glory, we will be the perverters of their hearts.

As the dearth of ethics and morality rise and the masses begin to seek protection, we will continue to offer security in carefully crafted emblems. Only to the simple mind can an object, a lifeless object created by their own kind, protect them from the supernatural, but they believe it, so we feed their fears. We use the cross in our symbols to bear the appearance of Christ-like religious innocence, then add our cultic emblems for special demonic overshadowing. We have spun the cross upside down, broken the ends, and placed it in an unending circle to represent the invalidity of Christ's death, then cleverly labeled it the peace sign. As they wear these emblems over their heart, we gain entry; when it is on the ear, we are able to speak without obstruction. We gleaned this idea when God told Moses to bear the names of the children of Israel over his heart.

While we will enjoy tremendous success from these seemingly insignificant plots, we will further secure a dead-bolt control over our greatest threat of all times, the Church. To date the most influential hold we have exerted over the Church is the use of the media. We have successfully transitioned the animated message carried by television into the homes of many believers and with our subliminal lies that filter into their minds, we have taken control, invading countless homes with lust, greed, and pride. Children are taught the art of disrespect and disobedience to parents through this wonderful means. We have closed territorial distances and influenced children to run away to seek their fortune and an easier life by desiring riches and fame. Principal spirits now control homes, yet they are smart enough to allow a measure of godliness so these homes can be deceived into thinking they are living for God— our coined title for them is *Sunday Morning Christians.*

Commander we currently have a functioning team whose job is to persuade and suck the church into our methods and strategy of growth, a contingency of evil that penetrates and controls the church from within. We convince the church into believing that their headcount and their bank accounts are their yardsticks of success. Once they buy into the notion, our spirits will be the principals and proprietors behind their master plan of achievement and growth. At that point, we do not have to conjure evil, we only need to control their minds, and influence their production and output while we saturate them with pride. They attain the understanding that the conglomerate is built by their own hands, and upon that confession, we become rightful owners of the entire flock.

As evil trendsetters, we allow them to copy patterns of evolving technology, then we mask it with a religious label and cover it with pride. Our spirits lodge deep within that which is produced for their God so we ultimately get the glory.

To attain the level of worldly success they seek, we will release finances from sources we know will strip them of purity—a corruption of compromise. This well-laid bait will be masked so carefully with promises of reaching souls, it will look like the genuine thing. It will be like looking through a mirror—the reflection is an exact replica which even the trained eye cannot detect—it would take spiritual discernment from the Holy Spirit, whom they would not possess.

Their entire Christmas celebrations will be virtually turned over to us. Every theme of Christmas will be loaded with six-point stars surrounded by a circle to represent the divine mind, a direct counterfeit of the Almighty's wisdom. These fanatics have gone so far from the heart of the Word, our job is easier than ever. God told them no statues—no created images because you will be led astray to idolize it in worship. He directly left no trace of His day of birth or death, or they would worship that too. So we have jazzed up all their celebrated holy days of worship, and each year, we enhance it with another creative emblem, which they feel pressured to collect.

Do you know they listen and obey us more than they do their God? It is hysterical, most of them have never heard Him and they do not seek out His presence. With us, it is easy. Add color, animate it, lay on some glitter or make it gory and intriguing to their fears, and we have a captive audience."

"You are a cocky little upstart, and you certainly have a lot to learn." The commander walked over to the principal with a wicked grin on his face.

"Do not get so conceited and sure of yourself. These plans of yours are not foolproof. God promised them that in times of ignorance, He will wink; so He will have mercy on whom He will have mercy. Let me quote, 'It is not him that wills or him that runs well, but it is of God to show mercy on whom He will.' So I am not as excited about your blindfold on the masses. That God we are dealing with will foil our strategy, He will turn it against us, but be certain, absolutely certain, that the only way to destroy a people is to destroy their leader. Attack leaders by corrupting their hearts, and certainly, as they follow your lead, they will bring the people under their curse. Then the entire drone belongs to me.

The competitive edge of a leader with laser-like vision is touted as the catalyst of success. That asset of strength must be converted into our model of destruction as we become their ultimate leader. In order for any leader to fail, he must be diverted from the protocols laid out for success. Strategic diversion which leads to failure is that which is poisoned by the glamour of Earth and mingled with the treachery of hell. Sell them promises you cannot keep, create lofty notions that only exist in hell, coerce them into seeing the Earth as their kingdom and your ideas of conquering as fulfilling, supply them with answers beyond their limited desires, and generate surrender.

Surrender is a weakness. Weakness is a discipline, and those who practice become perfect. Once the discipline of weakness is captured, retained, and fortified with glamour and selfish desire, you win.

My strategy is to address leaders of nations. Once that leader is eating out of my hands, the people will follow me gladly. Once that leader is intoxicated by my evil, the land is sucked into my spell. Even so, I am careful. The heart of man is boastful, so I carefully manage evil by balancing it with mammon. When an evil man is able to enjoy riches and honor, it does not matter to his heart if bodies are dropping like flies around him. That is when I am successful.

Again be very careful: if a man wears a symbol and is innocent of its meaning, you have no entry there. Therefore, until you can deliver blood into my hand, all your meticulously crafted symbols are a waste. Your ultimate strategy then is to become so influential to those who serve you that they deliver daily, and I mean daily: get them to deliver dead bodies to the door of hell. I have no gain in keeping man alive. I am not in the business of life, I am a mortician. I am only in the business of death, and I do not enjoy the dead who chose God. I do not gain from the death of God-fearing men. I want the dead bodies of those who are blindly ignorant of the truth of God and those who have served me faithfully, because I know He watches over each soul carefully, and at the tiniest plea for help He stretches out that loving hand to deliver them out of the darkest pit. My soul burns within me to know He did not give us a second chance. I just wanted a moment of glory; I wanted to be His Son. His love for His Son Jesus was so overwhelming it had us bowing in worship and adoration. Just once, I wanted it to be me. Only once, and I lost it all.

Arrrrggghhh. Mercy, mercy, mercy, even now, oh Mighty God, will You amend Your heart and have mercy on me. If only I could have another chance. I would give up my existence to just live at Your feet. Oh God, my God, my God."

"Out!" The foundation of the room erupted as he bellowed the insult. "Out, you imbeciles. Get out of my presence and get your work done. There is no mercy for those who make their bed in hell!"

CHAPTER 12

The Violent Take It by Force

Silence hovered over the town in the wee hours of the morning, but Angelique was restless. Gabe was kneeling at her bedside nudging her and whispering, "We need to put some extra time into this day—there is much ahead."

Finally she got out of bed and tiptoed down to the kitchen. Perhaps she would gain clarity over a cup of tea and a few coconut cookies. As she placed the kettle on the stove, she noted that the family Bible had been left open on the countertop. David must have been reading last night, she thought; however, it was Gabe who had prepared it for her. Attracted to the Book, she sat down to read. It was Psalm 68:

Let God arise, let His enemies be scattered: let them also that hate Him flee before Him. As smoke is driven away, so drive them away; as wax melts before the fire, so let the wicked perish at the presence of God. But let the righteous be glad, let them rejoice before God: yea, let them exceedingly rejoice. Sing unto God, sing praises to His name, extol Him that rides upon the heavens by His name Jah, and rejoice before Him. A father of the fatherless and a judge of the widows, is God in His holy habitation. God sets the solitary in families; He brings out those which are bound with chains: but the rebellious dwell in a dry land, O God, when Thou went forth before Thy people, when Thou didst march through the wilderness. Selah.

The earth shook, the heavens also dropped at the presence of God, even Sinai itself was moved at the presence of God, the God of Israel. Thou, O God, didst send a plentiful rain, whereby Thou didst confirm Thine inheritance, when it was weary. Thy congregation has dwelt therein, Thou O God, hast prepared of Thy goodness for the poor. The Lord gave the word, great was the company of those that published it.

Kings of armies did flee apace, and she that tarried at home divided the spoil. Though you have lien among the pots, yet shall you be as the wings of a dove covered with silver, and her feathers with yellow gold. When the Almighty scattered kings in it, it was white as snow in Salmon. The hill of God is as the hill of Bashan; an high hill as the hill of Bashan. Why leap ye, ye high hills? This is the hill which God desires to dwell in, yes, the Lord will dwell in it for ever. The chariots of God are twenty thousand, even thousands of angels, the Lord is among them, as in Sinai, in the holy place.

Thou has ascended on high, Thou has led captivity captive, Thou has received gifts for men; yea, for the rebellious also, that the Lord God might dwell among them. Blessed be the Lord, who daily loads us with benefits, even the God of our salvation. Selah.

He that is our God is the God of salvation, and unto God the Lord belong the issues from death. But God shall wound the head of His enemies, and the hairy scalp of such a one as goes on still in his trespasses. The Lord said, I will bring again from Bashan, I will bring My people again from the depths of the sea, that thy foot may be dipped in the blood of thine enemies, and the tongue of thy dogs in the same.

They have seen thy goings, O God, even the goings of my God, my King, in the sanctuary. The singers went before, the players on instruments followed after; among them were the damsels playing with timbrels. Bless ye God in the congregations, even the Lord, from the fountain of Israel. There is little Benjamin with their ruler, the princes of Judah and their council, the princes of Zebulun, and the princes of Naphtali. Thy God has commanded thy strength, strengthen O God, that which Thou hast wrought for us. Because of Thy temple at Jerusalem shall kings bring presents unto Thee.

Rebuke the company of spearmen, the multitude of the bulls, with the calves of the people, till every one submit himself with pieces of silver: scatter Thou the people that delight in war. Princes shall come out of Egypt; Ethiopia shall soon stretch out her hands unto God. Sing unto God, ye kingdoms of the earth, O sing praises unto the Lord. Selah.

To him that rides upon the heavens of heavens, which were of old, lo, He does send out His voice, and that a mighty voice. Ascribe you strength unto God, His excellency is over Israel, and His strength is in the clouds. O God, Thou art terrible out of Thy holy places, the God of Israel is He that giveth strength and power unto His people. Blessed be God.

"What are You saying to me, dear Lord?"

Gabe whispered, "This sounds like war; this sounds like an attack from the kingdom of darkness. You who ride upon the heavens, with a mighty voice, drive the enemy away. Rebuke the company of spearmen, as smoke is driven away, so drive them away: as wax melts before the fire, so let the wicked perish at the presence of God. The chariots of God are twenty thousand, even thousands of angels: the Lord is among them, as in Sinai, in the holy place."

The whistle from the kettle broke through her meditation. She rose to make the tea and saw David standing at the door.

"Darling, how long have you been there?"

He walked over and held her, his eyes preoccupied with his own thoughts. "I had a strange dream. You and I were in a courtroom and were being judged for serving the Lord. The man or the thing who brought the accusations against us was huge and diabolically ugly. Every time he opened his mouth to speak, you would raise your hand to the Lord and his speech became muffled. Eventually the judge got tired of his babbling and decided he would sentence us to death anyway. You held onto me and said, 'We will not die. David, agree with me, we will not die.'" In the far distance, way beyond the courtroom, I could see an army of men dressed in black coming to get us and together we began to cry out for the blood of Jesus to save us. I woke up screaming for the blood of Jesus."

Gabe whispered, "The message on Sunday."

"And I just read Psalm 68—Let God arise and His enemies be scattered. David, remember the message you preached on Sunday, 'Sanctify Yourselves for

Tomorrow the Lord Will Do Wonders Among You?' Let's sanctify ourselves, let's take of the Passover Cup."

The agreement was unanimous. He got the grape juice and she got the bread, then together they bowed their heads to seek the face of the Lord.

"Amazing God and our Father, who keeps covenants to a thousand generation, You have called us out of darkness into Your marvelous light, You have reserved us for Your work here on earth and we are Your willing servants. Father, the hour has come, sanctify us by Your word; Your word is true. Just like Jesus taught us to pray, lead us not into temptation but deliver us from evil, we ask that You deliver us from the accuser of our souls, and lead us not into the traps of hell. We yield our hearts, our souls, and our minds to You that You would wash us and cleanse us from all uncleanness, from the contamination of the weaknesses of the mind, from the filth of the flesh, and bring us into Your Presence covered in the blood of Your Son our Lord and Savior Jesus Christ.

Father, we desire to know Your heart and accomplish Your will; we desire to be Your heartbeat in the earth that the Church may experience Your glory revealed for the end time.

Father, these words which You have spoken to us in dreams and through Your holy Scriptures, we gather them with the anointing that resides in the Holy Spirit, and we call heaven in agreement to cancel the assignments of hell. Satan, the Lord God Almighty rebukes you. We declare confusion to your carefully laid plans, we cast down every high thing that exalts itself against the knowledge of God, and we bind principalities and powers, the rulers of the darkness of the age, might and dominion, and any name that is named against the will and the purposes of God.

We speak strength to the angels of the Most High God and declare catastrophe to the gates of hell. Jesus, You have given us revelation like that which was given to Your disciple Peter, and Lord, You declared that upon the revelation of the Spirit and the truth, the gates of hell will not prevail. Let not the gates of hell prevail against us Father. We know we are in a war for our very lives, and to the army of men dressed in black that have been sent to get us, we summon the hosts of heaven, and in agreement with the Word of God, we bind up every conceived plot; and to the assignments we speak complete and crippling failure that no evil shall come near our dwelling.

Father, we bless this bread to become the broken body of the Lord Jesus Christ, and we bless this drink to become His sacred blood, and as we partake, fulfill Your will in the Earth through the shed blood of the Lord Jesus Christ, and demolish the strongholds and the strongman; let the blood bring pardon to our lives that the accuser's tongue will be silenced. We stand under the scepter of the righteousness of our Lord God, under the banner of Christ's Love, and just like Pharaoh's army pursued Your people to their own demise, so we pray that You will destroy this army, horsemen and riders, and weapons and strategies. Reroute our plans Father, give us understanding and wisdom to listen and apply Your heart as You unfold Your knowledge to us that we may ultimately say, *The Lord our God has given us the victory.* Father, bring the healing and grace we so desperately long for, bring the wealth of Your knowledge that keeps our minds stayed on You, and bring the prophetic utterance that will lead us into the will of Your heart and out of the paths of destruction.

Father, thank You for opening our eyes in visions and dreams, and thank You for visiting our home with Your Holy Spirit. We are humbled that You have chosen us to be Your children, and with all our hearts, we want to honor that call. So Heavenly Father, teach us how to love You with all our hearts instead of loving and satisfying ourselves, that we may apply our hearts unto wisdom. We bless You and thank You for giving ear to our prayer and delivering us from evil in the Name of Jesus Christ our Lord we pray. Amen."

"Ask the Lord for divine and angelic covering for David." Gabe's voice was gentle, but she knew it well.

Angelique pulled her chair closer to David and rested her head on his chest. She loved to listen to the thump of his heart. For a few seconds she lay there just listening, trying to detect the rhythm it made. "Do you know that I love you more than anyone in this whole wide world?"

A huff of laughter changed the rhythm of his heartbeat. "I have had my challenges, but you have indeed been faithful. I must say, these past few weeks have been pleasantly wonderful, and yet I have no real explanation. I could attribute my softened heart to the excitement of our weekend getaway, but I know that's not it, because my prayers have increased, the language of my prayers have been stronger and more targeted, and I have a sense of urgency to draw closer to God." He began stroking her fingers. "Now, all of that has made you the most beautiful gem in my eyes. You, my darling, are a most gorgeous work of art, God spared nothing in fashioning your contours, making you delightfully pleasing to my eyes."

Warm tears slid down her cheeks as she basked in the tenderness of his words. "Father, thank You for my husband—thank You for this man of God that You have provided to share my life. Lord, I love Your son, I love this man, and I ask You to cover him with the blood of Your Son the Lord Jesus Christ. Holy Spirit, wash David's heart. Go into the recesses of his mind, and purify every part. I sanctify him wholly unto You Father God, and now I petition the Holy Spirit to enter into his heart and close the door: seal it, render it impermeable to any other spirit. Holy Spirit, cover my husband's mind with the mind of Christ, so he will know and obey the voice of God only. Protect us from all harm and danger, Lord: protect this town, and cover all these towns all the way to the city. Father, stretch the palm of Your hand over us and deliver us from every plan of darkness. Let not sin have dominion over us, for You, oh Sovereign Lord, are God alone. Amen.

Remember to assign him an angel. The insistent voice was gentle.

"David, David, one more thing!" She raised her head and turned to face him, then she placed her hand on his head. "Heavenly Father, David and I agree that there will be an angel of God, sent from the realms of glory to be David's partner. Father, choose a warrior, a strategist, a builder, and an angel of great rank and authority. We thank You, Lord, and are indeed grateful that You hear and answer our prayers. Now we seal all these words with the blood of this Passover Cup, and give them to our angels to bear them up to

You that You may bless these words and return them to the Earth with Your signature of approval as they accomplish Your will in the Earth. Empower the angels to fight, Father, give them a winning strategy. Give them access to the plans of hell; I declare that wisdom and understanding be poured out that the battle may be fought in the spirit and not come down to Earth; I declare miracles being performed on Earth as a sign of Your divine protection; I declare a prophetic utterance for the saints to be covered and not touched or harmed by evil; and I declare victory to every soldier that stands to fight for the Lord, in Jesus' Name. Amen.

"Amen. Just the prayers we needed. Welcome Daniel, I am glad you were chosen."

"I have been petitioning for this position, but I had to wait until I got the invitation. I'm excited, looking forward to this weekend." Daniel was a strong angel with huge wings. His face glowed with excitement, and Gabe knew he could be trusted.

"Well, I want you to take them away. You may encounter turbulence, but we have a mapped out route."

David held up the bread. "The body of the Lord Jesus Christ: let us eat." They both held onto the bread and broke it together, then bowed their heads in silence as they ate.

"Our Lord said this is His blood which was shed for the remission of sins. Here we find pardon, cleansing, strength, wholeness, salvation, and peace. Father, let this cup be a token of Your will being done on Earth even as it is perfectly executed in heaven. Let us drink of the blood of our Lord Jesus Christ." He placed the glass to her lips and smiled as her heart-shaped lips parted to drink of the Cup. He finished the rest and they bowed their heads in silence as they customarily did.

"Darling, I have one of my spontaneous ideas. Can we leave today? Can you get leave from your job? I am eager to go."

"David, ahhh!" She was playful in her tone. "Ok, let me go in today and see if I can leave early. I will have to get coverage for these two days."

"We should have left two weeks ago—we are overdue."

"Daniel, have you been briefed on the weekend plans."

"Yes, I have been following every detail carefully."

"There has to be a change of plans. Have David reschedule the weekend stay to Great Isle. Several attacks have been planned for the present location. Ask him to give the weekend at Surf Bay to John and his wife. John has been slated to have a nervous breakdown while cleaning this weekend, and trigger an electrical failure which will set the building on fire. Let's whisk him away.

Here is a small list of things that need to be taken care of today. Top of the list, Mother Hubbard will be going into the hospital today with a mild heart attack. David must not hear about it. It will be taking place around the eleventh hundred hour. He must be in the shower when the phone call comes in or distracted somehow. If he knows, Angelique will hear of it, and the weekend will be instantly postponed. Mother Hubbard has been given a complementary stay at the hospital, so her grandson's visit will be thrown back to the dogs.

Second, Angelique will want to stop and get lunch at her favorite restaurant, I want them engaged in new revelation and insight to new spiritual concepts so she will forget to indulge her taste buds. Traps are set all along the old route. Another idea is to stage a buildup of traffic leading up to that route and divert them around town.

I must stay to fight for Adia; her father has been crying out for her, and she does not have an assigned angel. She still considers Angelique her best friend, so I have some authority to fight for her. I will ride with you out to the highway and we should have this town all cleared by the time you get back. If you are in need of anything, ask Angelique. She is sharply attuned to the Father and will pray your requests into action. Don't forget to have her honor her daily times of prayer—we will need that for this weekend's battle. In fact, we are removing their physical bodies from the war zone, but the purpose of the getaway is to intercede for the town.

Follow this list until I bring Angelique back from the hospital. We are going to experience an attack there, but she is prepared. Please alert David to it so he can cover her in prayer. Angelique is ready. Thanks, partner."

She got into her car and started the engine and like clockwork her heart began to pray.

"Why not pray in tongues?"

"Yes I should." The words flowed from her lips as she backed the car out of the garage.

"I enter by the blood of the Lamb..." Her favorite radio station was playing her favorite song by Paul Wilbur. She joined in.

"Lord, I worship You, I worship You. Lord I worship You, I worship You. For Your Name is Holy, Holy, Lord. For Your name is Holy, Holy, Lord." The violin escalated the divine melody to produce a heavenly sound.

"I enter the Holy of holies, I enter by the blood of the Lamb. I enter to worship You only, I enter to honor I am. Lord I worship You. I worship You. Lord I worship You. I worship You. For Your name is Holy, Holy, Lord. For Your name is Holy, Holy, Lord." The violin brought the song to its tapered ending. The holiness of the moment resounded inside her heart, and she began to worship her God.

"Ask that your request for time off be granted, and request the supernatural protection of many angels for today." They had developed a beautiful line of communication. He heard from God, passed it on to her, she spoke the words in prayer, he ushered it back to God, and boom, like a flash of light, it was done.

"Dear Lord, please grant me favor to receive these days away from work and I pray divine protection for David and myself today. Release more angels to cover us. I ask for a divine release of many angels to keep guard around us today. Release battalions of angels in this town, Lord. Bring them in with drawn swords and station them strategically throughout this region. I speak strength and victory to the angels of God as they battle for the souls of Your people. Thwart every plan of hell, discover the secrets hidden in dark places, and expose the tactics of evil; upset the cart of trouble planned against Your people, and set the face of evil against itself to destroy its kingdom from within. Father, let the Earth know how much You love her, let the people know how much You care; let each heart draw near to Your heart with full assurance of faith, believing and trusting in the Lord God Almighty; let us lay aside every weight and the sin which so easily beset us, and let us run with patience the race that is set before us, for the joy of entering into Your gates with thanksgiving and into Your courts with praise. Lord, take us on a new experience with You, not so we would have what to brag about, but that we might be pulled into the treasure of fellowship and joys of our Lord, that we might experience the power and absolute joys of unity found only in You. Father, what is it like for two to become one? Teach me the perfection and splendor of unity, of becoming one with David and with Your Holy Spirit."

It was early morning and the parking lot had lots of great parking spaces. She pulled in, deep in thought. David had been freed from the burden of perfecting the church. She had labored before God for years to teach him the beauty of trust. It is God who builds the church, he had to place the reigns of control in God's hand and enjoy the ride of taking orders. Definitely, he had relinquished the control. "I pray that spirit will be bound in the pits, never to return."

"Ms. Angelique, you are early." Mya was bubbly.

"A pleasant good morning to you too, my dear." Her words were glazed with her smile.

"We had a great night, peaceful, no frantic calls, really great."

"Mya, I wanted to see about changing a few shifts. I need to take two extra days, and I need coverage."

"Lauren was asking for a few more hours this week as she will be out to see her parents next week, and I will gladly cover for you anytime, Ms. Angelique."

"Ok, let me go to my office and change the schedule. I will call Lauren with the details. Also, I will make a few rounds before I leave this morning."

She started walking to her office.

"Tell Mya how precious she is."

Angelique smiled. She turned and headed back.

"Mya!"

"Yes, Ms. Angelique?"

"It is such a pleasure having you here on staff. You are indeed a blessing to this hospital and to me. Thank you."

Mya blushed, then used her first finger to remove the tear that showed her gratitude. Angelique smiled and turned again to go to her office. As she sat at her desk, an overwhelming sense of urgency sat down with her.

"Lord, what must I do?"

"Let the plans of God unfold, only pray for divine protection."

"Thank you Lord, for divine protection. Let Your plans unfold Heavenly Father, I am yours."

She got up and made herself a cup of tea, then sat down to get her work straightened out so it would be easy for Mya to follow when she was gone. Three hours later, she placed her pen in its holder, closed her file drawer, and decided to go and bring some cheer to her patients. Across from her office was Mrs. Carver, a wonderful old lady who had suffered a fractured hip while alone at home.

"Good morning, Mrs. Carver, how are you feeling this morning?"

"Oh dear, dear. Oh, it is indeed a lovely day. Oh dear, how are you?"

Angelique reached out to her hands. They were warm and soft, milky soft.

"I am doing well. The question is how are you? Are you ready to go home?"

"Oh my darling, you know I like it here. I'm so alone at home, the children are gone and I have nobody, there is no one to talk with. Sarah packed up and left; by the way, she phoned to say it is wonderful with that daughter of hers, and I am, well, I have no one."

"Any pain?"

"No, no pain. Just in my head, I am really trying to sort out this whole plan. I wish I knew what to do."

"Ok, Mrs. Carver, I will be praying for something great to work in your favor."

"Thank you, dear, thank you."

Angelique kissed her hand and inched her way out.

As she stepped into the hall, a wave of caution swept over her. She slowed her pace but proceeded to see Mr. Stark. She nodded to the police officers, and with her cheerful voice announced her good morning.

The bed shook and rattled, the chains clanked. In what seemed like a blink of the eye, his body was in the air and lunging towards her.

She screamed. "Noooooooo, Jesus, nooo, Jesus, Jesus."

Gabe skated ahead of her and punched the monster to the floor then quickly refastened the chain on Mr. Stark's right leg, and smoothly with a lightening turn, flashed his sword to deflect the oncoming bullet.

Pop, pop. She felt the heat of the bullet as it whisked pass her face and through the sodium solution hanging from the pole, and into the wall.

The chain on his right leg still clutched to the rail as he growled viciously, rolling back and forth with the strength of a lion.

Screams came from everywhere. A hand grabbed her by the waist and carried her out into the hall, where the commotion was as chaotic.

The police guard held her in his hands like a baby, "Nurse, are you all right? Did you get hurt? Nurse, nurse, speak to me."

Gabe whispered, "Take her to Room 788 at the far end of the hall."

She lay in the hospital bed, dazed by the activity, replaying the scene over and over in her head. It was not the shock of the bullet or Mr. Stark's violent outburst, her subconscious understanding grappled with the events and refused to believe she was the target of such a violent attack. The doctor was as frightened as she was. He instantly ordered a leave of absence and informed her that David was on his way to pick her up.

What was this war about? David had that dream early this morning, and she had the dream about the children a few days ago; were they all pieces of the puzzle? Oh, and the Psalm she read this morning, 'Let God arise and His enemies be scattered," and the verse that said 'He would protect the fatherless.'

"Oh God, my God, my shield and strength and present help in times of trouble. A thousand shall fall at my side, and ten thousand at my right hand, but they shall not touch me. Therefore I will not fear, though the mountains shake with the swelling thereof and the waters roar and are troubled. Where is that Scripture, where is my purse?"

As she swung her feet down to get up from the bed, she heard the door slowly creaking, opening. He heart shot into her throat as fear closed out the air from her lungs. It was David.

"Oh God!" She burst out in tears and ran to him.

"My sweetheart, how are you? I heard. I was so frightened I could hardly control myself while driving. How are you?"

Her voice was inaudible through the sobs, and her legs did not wish to use their muscles anymore. David scooped her up and squeezed her body to his.

"Thank You, Lord, for protecting my bride. Father, thank You. Honey, let's get out of here. It doesn't feel right in here; a strong sense of fear has taken over this place, and I want to get out of its path."

He lowered her feet to the floor while holding her gently, guiding her out. He opened the car door and helped her to get in then gently squeezed her hand as he nuzzled her face with his lips.

Neither of them had words for the trauma she had just experienced. "I made a change of plans, we are going to Great Isle. I thought since we have two more days we could take advantage of the beach there." He looked over at her, wanting to cheer her spirit. "This will make you happy. I gave the reservation at Surf Bay to John and Crystal."

She was silent, responding only with a faint smile.

"Is a penny enough to share those deep thoughts?" Her eyes were closed and he was not sure if she was in pain or shock. "Nope, not enough? Two pennies, three?" He reached over and held her hand. "I could not live without you, and I am so grateful that God protected you when I could not."

She tilted her head backward and sighed. "I felt so scared, but when you held me, it all went away. I have never felt more secure and happy than that moment I saw you."

Daniel whispered from the back seat. "No need to go back to the house, you have everything you need to leave town."

"Let's get out of town. Let's go find each other." David's voice was hoarse with desire.

Gabe was riding on the top, sword drawn, carefully watching his territory. "Daniel, remind Angelique of the Psalm, and have her read it to David. There is nothing present now, but the house is being watched carefully. I will take you out to the highway. You should be safe from there." Gabe's sword was out of its sheath and glinting in the sun as a deterrent to any that would dare stage an attack. He was taking no chances. They did not know of the change of plans to Great Isle; not even Martha knew, and he wanted to keep it that way.

"Please have David pray the prayer of protection, send him an urgent message. I want to be sure it is completed before I take leave."

David heard the instructions and started to pray. "Father, my heart is grateful; You snatched my wife out of danger, You covered her with Your life. Thank you Lord, we depend on You and You have never failed us. Now, Father, let the life of God manifest its glory in us as we travel. We ask for the protective covering of the blood of our Lord Jesus Christ. Destroy the works of darkness; every foul plan, every evil work, every word spoken against us, we demolish by the resurrection power that raised Christ from the dead. Now unto Him who is able to do exceedingly, abundantly, above all that we ask or think according to the power that works in us; for we are complete in Him, hidden in Christ Jesus through faith, quickened and made alive in our mortal bodies by the Holy Spirit that dwells in us, and risen by faith through the working of the knowledge of God: unto the all-wise God be glory and honor and praise, forever. Amen."

"Amen. Daniel, I bless you in the Name of our Lord. I will join you soon. Angelique, you are not alone, God will never let you down, because you are the apple of His eye. Keep praying because we are strengthened by your prayers." He flew off.

Daniel climbed onto the roof and assumed the position of guardianship.

Gabe headed towards Adia's home; he was summoned by her father and the prayers were reinforced by Angelique. The atmosphere was charged with Fear and Frustration, but he knew they were not the spirits he needed to address. He soared higher to view the complete layout.

"I knew you were coming; great to work with you again."

Gabe spun in the air, wheeling his sword to ward off any possible assault.

"In exchange for a bit of divine protection for my dear Adia, I can provide you with all the details you need to secure your turf."

"I will make no deals with you. I have a job to do, and God is well able to take care of His own."

"Did you know about the train wreck planned for Friday morning and the explosion in the tunnel during the evening commute? Did you know we are using the old stone church outside Londonsville as a base and staging an all-out attack on the town, including burning the sanctuary early Sunday morning?"

"Will you release Adia to the Lord?"

"Well, I should not lie to an angel of the Most High God, so how can I bargain to keep her and still get your protection?"

"Again, Norion, I do not make bargains with hell."

"Technically, I am on your team now. I am here at your service to work for you."

"Release your hold on Adia so I can minister life to her."

"I could go down and clear the air of all the imps surrounding her so you can have full access for ministry."

"Release your hold."

"Gabe, we have staged an attack at Angelique's favorite restaurant in about an hour. Would you like me to help you defend her? They are on their way to Surf Bay and our commander will be there to stage an accident to kill David."

Gabe pushed off through the air ignoring the advice and the offering of sin. Norion glided off behind him.

"Well, it so happens that my assignment was upstaged and Boulog was sent to take Adia home. She is fair game Gabe, nobody owns her. She is yours for the asking." He shouted the information as Gabe slipped into the invisible.

Fury boiled in his blood; he was betrayed by the god he served and ignored by the angel of the Almighty. He was an outsider. That's it, he would defend his property and destroy every demon in hell if he had to. The parlor had an underground entry from the basement. He slipped in unnoticed and hid himself in Charles Buckenshide. From there, he scanned the house. Boulog had invited a host of sickening ghouls to the feast and they were crawling around everywhere. Adia was curled up under a blanket with the shroud spread on top. Fever was curled up with her. If Fever saw him, it would spoil his game. He would summon her mother to get some alcohol and drive Fever away. He got out of Charles and started to tiptoe into the kitchen.

Whoosh! Clang! Pling!

"Get off me!"

"Ouch, my leg is broken."

"Help, twist my face back into place!"

The complaints were never ending. The host of demons that possessed Adia's house were being slashed left and right and being thrown into chains. Adia's father had just arrived, and as he looked at the daughter he was forced to abandon, he cried out for mercy and deliverance from the plagues that had her bound. He kneeled beside her on the couch and removed the old musty bloodstained blanket, throwing it into the trash basket.

He continued to pray. "Father, cover my baby with the blood of Jesus Christ, and wash away the deeds of darkness. I bind up principalities and powers and the hosts of wickedness that have possessed her soul. Spirits of darkness, I bind you in the Name of Jesus Christ, free my daughter from the hold you possess over her. Every generational curse, the spells and incantations she has channelled into her life, the blood sacrifices, the offerings to the dark world, the many souls that she has bound in chains to attain the ranking of spiritual success, the lies and deceit and the years of giving her soul unto darkness, I strip away by faith through the blood of Jesus Christ my Lord. Come, Holy Spirit, come and minister to my daughter now."

"Dad, do you really believe God will hear you?" Her eyes were weak, and her faint voice was full of hope and doubt.

"Darling, I know He does."

"Would He listen to me if I talked to Him?"

Her father smiled while tears flowed from his eyes. He opened his mouth to speak, but the tears had choked him up.

"Lord, I am ready to give up a lifetime of evil and deception if You will have me. I am so sorry, so sorry for the things I have done. Can You help me make it right? Lord, can You deliver those I have committed to the hand of darkness, the souls I have led astray, can You heal us, Lord? I am ready to trust You. Please forgive me of my sins, come and live in my heart, and I will give You my life forever."

Her father drew closer and hugged her, praying and crying and smiling all at once.

"What is going on?"

"Mamma, Mamma, Jesus helped me."

Her mother froze. The look on her face registered doubt and anxiety.

"Dad helped me. Come he can help us, he knows how to say powerful prayers." She rose to escort her mother to the couch. Her father bowed his head and used his hands to shield his eyes. Her mother walked over and sat between them.

"Joseph, I am not sure I can believe this thing. I have trusted the healing my parents taught me all my life—if I give a little, I will get a little."

"Mable, you have secured help for this life, but how will you navigate the plains of death? What of your soul?"

"I don't know the truth about death. Does anyone really know?"

"You will know the truth when you have met the God of love. He gives us assurance in our hearts as we surrender to Him."

"Joseph, I am sorry that I drove you away. I took Adia from you in my selfishness because I wanted Margo to feel like my life was just like hers. I lied about you and made your life miserable. I am sorry."

He glided his hand around her waist and pulled her to his warmth.

"I never stopped loving you. I never stopped loving Adia, and I vowed someday you would be my wife again. When I left, I found Christ, and He strengthened my heart. I have prayed for this moment."

Gabe whispered, "Lead her to Christ."

"Will you accept Jesus Christ as your Lord and Savior?"

"I am not sure of it all, but I trust you, and so I will."

"Thank you, Joseph. I will leave a host of angels to surround this house. Will you stay here for a few days to secure the bonds?"

"Mable, Adia, I know this is a little premature but can I come home? I would love to stay tonight as well."

Mable hugged him. Adia leaned on her mother. The tears were loud in the heavens as repentance and healing tolled their bells of victory.

Gabe threw his sword into the air, and as it twirled back into his hand, he shouted, "Hallelujah!"

Mother Hubbard was on her knees at her altar, tears streaming down her face as she cried out to the Lord for His continued favor on His children.

"Gabe, I have been waiting, everything is ready." Shoer's excitement was contagious. "All the prayers have gone up, and now she is basking in the warmth of the fellowship of the Holy Spirit."

"Bid her call her daughter."

Mother Hubbard heard the direction and struggled to raise herself from her knees. She fetched a napkin and wiped her eyes as she walked to the phone.

She dialed and waited. "Coletta, my darling, how are you?" She waited while her daughter filled her in.

"Imagine that! I was just praying and the Lord told me to call you." More silence.

"Shoer, now! Inflict pain that simulates a heart attack; don't affect the heart."

"Yes sir."

Mother Hubbard started to cough and an unbearable pain started in her chest. "Coletta, Col... my heart... pain. Call the doctor." Her hand began to tremble and she dropped the phone.

"Ok, we will wait." He paced around the room. "Please prop her up so she is comfortable." His pacing was becoming uneasy. "Speak to her heart and keep her calm, I will go get the ambulance." He was out in a flash.

His flight was hurried, and his eyes were vigilant, scanning the town as he went.

"Gabe, quick! David and Angelique were attacked."

The sound of the news ruffled his ears and upset his flight. He spun in the air with such velocity that the clouds were pulled together from all angles, clashing together to produce the effect of lightening.

"Tell me they are not hurt!"

"David is deathly hurt."

"Jesus, Jesus, Jesus!" His cry got so loud, thunders were heard below.

"Assist Shoer with Mother Hubbard. Thank you for bringing the news." He was off in a flash.

The rescue team was lifting David out of the wreckage. His head was badly damaged and bleeding internally. Control with seven other demons more wicked than himself was strategically staged at the scene. Angelique was crying hysterically but did not have any bruises.

He halted outside the scene and called for back-up. He had to get Angelique to set aside her emotions and begin prayer for the accident. He sent her messages, and he could tell she received them but the atmosphere was so charged with other spirits, it was a challenge to begin the prayer. He needed back up for this fight.

They were indeed headed to Great Isle, so the plans for Surf Bay were thrown into confusion. However, Control had come back to take up residence in David, plus he brought reinforcement. Once he entered, David lapsed back into his old familiar pattern, giving Control full authority to play his foul game. This was the result, and it seemed as if they were merciless, because David's head trauma was severe. Daniel must have been cast out by David's words because he was nowhere in sight. If that were true, there was no angelic covering for either David or Angelique when Control and his host of spiritual wickedness came to do their dirty deeds.

Sirens and cars were everywhere. Oh great, his backup team was arriving in some of the rescue squad cars. He jumped into the back seat of the first car and hailed his fellow angel. Each angel understood the drill to perform the spiritual rescue—it did not have to be spoken. As the cars screeched to a stop, each angel transformed himself into light and slipped under the collars and sleeves of each of the rescue team. From there they would coax the team into the righteous handling of the accident.

"Ma'am, how are you, are you in pain?" The officer knelt before Angelique and Gabe got his chance to transfer to Angelique's sleeve while the other angel remained with the officer. He preferred her sleeves as her hands were so often clasped in prayer. Even through the many interruptions of Fear, he was able to comfort her and help her in times of prayer.

She raised her hand as a gesture of "I don't know" when Gabe spoke.

"Will you help me pray Officer? I am fine but my husband is wounded. If we pray, we can salvage him from this wreckage."

The officer's face registered a puzzling smile. He shook his head. "I have been on this beat for over twenty years, and your response has been the most shocking." The angel under his collar spoke to him.

"It wouldn't hurt."

"But it wouldn't hurt, now, would it?"

Angelique extended her hand to him. "Heavenly Father, forgive us, for we have sinned, and the wrath of the spirits of darkness have manifested their deeds upon us. But You, oh all mighty God are able to send reinforcement of angels even now to shred to pieces the realms of darkness and turn this evil into good. Father, we repent, remove evil far from us and heal

David from any damage brought to him. Free Your son from the hold of sin; free him from the spirits that so familiarly take control of his life. I stand in the gap for my husband, and I bind up principalities and powers and every name that is named, and I cast them out of him and declare defeat to the works and plans of evil. Set us free, Lord, please Father, set us free by the blood our Lord and Savior Jesus Christ. Amen."

"Amen."

Light beamed up from the accident scene, and swords began clanking and plunking. Gabe took on Control with such fury the beast was frightened by his might. Control was taken aback for just a moment, but whirled and lunged at Gabe. Gabe darted and Control's sword plunged into the heart of Lust. He tried to shake off the beast, but was not fast enough because Gabe pinned Lust to the face of Control while his sword twisted through his neck. In a flash, he bound both of them in chains and rolled them thousands of miles out into the air. He turned to view the battle, every demon in view was either bound or severely wounded. He swirled around the battlefield with the chain in his hand, shouting, "The blood of Jesus, the blood." All the fighting angels knew the sound well. The battle cry meant victory was won—prepare your victims for chains. Each angel echoed the cry, "The blood of Jesus, the blood of Jesus," as they knotted their victims in chains and cast them out.

Gabe stopped, planted one foot on an invisible pedestal, and sighed, "That's the effect of fervent prayer."

He beckoned to the angels as he trailed off to get into the ambulance. Angelique was by David's side.

He examined the casualty. It was a stage level-ten accident. Control had intended to sacrifice David in this battle to earn favor in the eyes of his commander so he could be granted another territory. He wanted David dead on the spot.

"David, wake up. Death needs your permission to take you. Do not give up—I need you here. I cannot go on without you, your time is not up. I am fighting for you, but I need you to agree with me, not with death. Look into my eyes, David, look into my eyes." Her voice roared in his subconscious and his eyelids raised themselves with all the strength they could muster. "Agree with me now: *say it*, I will not die."

His lips fumbled an unintelligible agreement, and he faded off to sleep.

BOOK 2
A Book of Prayers

The Model Prayer Jesus Taught

Our Father who lives in Heaven, holy and sacred is Your name. Lord Your kingdom has come, now let Your will be done in our lives here on Earth, in the same fluent manner it is done and carried out in Heaven. Give us this day our daily bread, and forgive us our sins even as we forgive those who have sinned against us, and lead us not into temptation but deliver us from all evil. For the Kingdom belongs to You, all power and all glory belongs to You, forever and ever. *Amen.*

Prayer of Confidence Psalm 23

The Lord is my shepherd, I shall not want. He makes me to lie down in green pastures, He leads me beside still waters, He restores my soul. He leads me in the paths of righteousness, for His name's sake. Yes, though I walk through the valley of the shadow of death, I will fear no evil, for You are with me, Your rod and staff will comfort me. You prepare a table before me in the presence of mine enemies, You anoint my head with oil, my cup runs over. Surely goodness and mercy shall follow me all the days of my life and I will dwell in the house of the Lord forever. *Amen.*

A Prayer for God's Will

Heavenly Father, who is honored above all and is in all, I come to Your throne by faith. Holy God, You are the first and the last, the beginning and the end, You are the author and the finisher of my faith.

I surrender all I am to You and ask that the characteristics and the nature of God will be mine today. Lead me by Your Holy Spirit, making me sensitive and obedient, following diligently, attentively, earnestly, and sincerely. Let my senses and my spirit be fully tuned to You that I will not be led off course or become distracted by anything.

Thank You Lord for sealing this prayer with Your love, in Jesus Christ's name I pray. *Amen.*

The Word of Faith

Matchless and holy Lamb of God who loved me and gave Himself for me, hear the petition of my heart.

My heart is being tested and soul is burdened by it. Holy One, I ask now for a word from the heart of God, for instructions that will bring deliverance or break the bonds that brought about this test.

I will implement Your word by faith and allow the word to create faith in my spirit. *Amen.*

Prayer of Repentance from Deceitful Patterns

Father God, I repent of the lies and the deceit which I have allowed to corrupt my life. I have generated patterns of uncleanness and selfishness that have taken hold of my heart.

Wash me clean, redeem me by the blood of Jesus Christ my Savior, deliver me for the curses I have brought on myself and the death that has infused itself into my life.

I now turn away from the works of evil and sin, I turn away from all that is not pleasing in Your eyes, I turn away looking to Your word and truth for guidance and to the love of Your heart that has drawn me to You.

Teach me to trust You Lord for everything and not to believe that my surrender is weakness, because I know how easy it was to submit to the patterns of darkness; now Father give me the strength to push past every evil desire and every carefully laid pattern and surrender my life to You.

Please watch over me and teach me to love You like You have loved me, in Jesus' Name. *Amen.*

Prayer in Times of Trouble Psalm 27

The Lord is my light and my salvation, whom shall I fear? The Lord is the strength of my life, of whom shall I be afraid? When the wicked, even mine enemies and my foes, came upon me to eat up my flesh, they stumbled and fell. Though a host should encamp against me, my heart shall not fear: though war should rise against me, in this will I be confident.

One thing have I desired of the Lord, that will I seek after; that I may dwell in the house of the Lord all the days of my life, to behold the beauty of the Lord, and to enquire in His temple. For in the time of trouble He shall hide me in His pavilion, in the secret of His tabernacle shall He hide me, He shall set me up upon a rock. And now shall mine head be lifted up above mine enemies round about me. Therefore will I offer in His tabernacle sacrifices of joy; I will sing, yea, I will sing praises unto the Lord.

Hear, O Lord, when I cry with my voice, have mercy also upon me, and answer me. When You said, Seek ye My face; my heart said unto You, Your face, Lord, will I seek. Hide not Your face far from me, put not Your servant away in anger. You have been my help, leave me not, neither forsake me, O God of my salvation. When my father and my mother forsake me, then the Lord will take me up.

Teach me Your way, O Lord, and lead me in a plain path, because of mine enemies. Deliver me not over unto the will of mine enemies: for false witnesses are risen up against me, and such as breathe out cruelty. I had fainted, unless I had believed to see the goodness of the Lord in the land of the living. Wait on the Lord, be of good courage, and He shall strengthen thine heart; wait, I say, on the Lord.

Prayer of Confidence for Children Psalm 8

O Lord, our Lord, how excellent is Your Name in all the earth! Who hast set Your glory above the heavens. Out of the mouth of babes and sucklings You have ordained strength because of Your enemies, that You might still the enemy and the avenger.

When I consider Your heavens, the work of Your fingers, the moon and the stars, which You have ordained, what is man, that thou are mindful of him, and the son of man, that You visit him? For You have made him a little lower than the angels, and hast crowned him with glory and honor. You made him to have dominion over the works of Your hands; You have put all things under his feet, all sheep and oxen, yea, and the beasts of the field, the fowl of the air, and the fish of the sea, and whatsoever passeth through the paths of the seas. O Lord our Lord, how excellent is Your name in all the earth!

A Prayer of Warfare Psalm 29

Give unto the Lord, O you mighty, give unto the Lord glory and strength. Give unto the Lord the glory due unto His name, worship the Lord in the beauty of holiness. The voice of the Lord is upon the waters, the God of glory thunders, the Lord is upon many waters. The voice of the Lord is powerful, the voice of the Lord is full of majesty. The voice of the Lord breaks the cedars, yea, the Lord breaks the cedars of Lebanon. He makes them also to skip like a calf, Lebanon and Sirion like a young unicorn. The voice of the Lord divides the flames of fire. The voice of the Lord shakes the wilderness; the Lord shakes the wilderness of Kadesh. The voice of the Lord makes the hinds to calve, and discovers the forests, and in His temple doth every one speak of His glory. The Lord sits upon the flood, yea, the Lord sits King for ever. The Lord will give strength unto His people, the Lord will bless His people with peace.

A Prayer for Mercy

Lord lift up the light of Your countenance upon us and grant us Your mercy. Your counsels are right O Lord, Your judgements are true.

I have been broken, my soul is in distress. I have not looked to Your word because my eyes have looked away. Show me Your ways oh Lord, teach me Your paths. Lead me in Your truth and teach me, for You are the God of My salvation, on You I wait all day.

Let Your truth cover me, let Your mercy cover me, let Your grace be my staff; I wait on You O Lord, for mercy. *Amen.*

Prayer to Break the Curse of the Violations of Blood

Heavenly Father, creator of the Heavens and the Earth, You alone are the sovereign God, there is none beside You, none above You, none like unto You. By Your words the Heaven and the Earth were created and because of You we have hope and a future against the realms of darkness that seek to deceive us into the patterns of death.

Father, every time we violate the use of blood the enemy makes a request for our souls. The accuser of our souls is legalistic but we know he has no authority except that it is given to him of God. Therefore Father we repent of every spiritual violation we have committed against You and Your word. We ask for the covenant of Jesus' blood upon our hearts. We know our Lord carries us in His heart and provides grace and mercy through the covenant which causes God our Father to extend love even when we have broken the covenant.

We cover our minds with the blood of Jesus Christ by faith. Do not let our minds take us where You are not leading Lord, and where You lead, please let our ears hear, our hearts understand, and our wills follow obediently. Where You lead, with authority, let us cover that ground in the covenant that it may yield all its increase for Your glory. Lord meet with us at the altar and teach us Your sovereignty and Your holiness that we may bow in worship to You our Holy God. In Jesus' Name we pray. *Amen.*

Memory Nuggets
A Nugget A Day, Keeps The Evil Away

Come unto Me, all you that labour and are heavy laden, and I will give you rest. Take My yoke upon you, and learn of Me; for I am meek and lowly in heart: and you shall find rest unto your souls. *Matthew 11:28-29*

If you faint in the day of adversity, your strength is small. *Proverbs 24:10*

And Jabez was more honorable than his brethren, and his mother called his name Jabez, saying, Because I bare him with sorrow. And Jabez called on the God of Israel, saying, Oh that Thou wouldest bless me indeed, and enlarge my coast, and that Thine hand might be with me, and that thou wouldest keep me from evil, that it may not grieve me! And God granted him that which he requested. *1 Chronicles 4:9-10*

Therefore also now, saith the Lord, turn you even to Me with all your heart, and with fasting, and with weeping, and with mourning: and rend your heart, and not your garments, and turn unto the Lord your God: for He is gracious and merciful, slow to anger, and of great kindness, and repents Him of the evil. Who knows if He will return and repent, and leave a blessing behind Him; even a meat offering and a drink offering unto the Lord Your God?

Blow the trumpet in Zion, sanctify a fast, call a solemn assembly; gather the people, sanctify the congregation, assemble the elders, gather the children, and those that suck the breasts: let the bridegroom go forth of his chamber, and the bride out of her closet, let the priests, the ministers of the Lord, weep between the porch and the altar, and let them say, Spare Your people, O Lord, and give not Your heritage to reproach, that the heathen should rule over them. Wherefore should they say among the people, Where is their God? Then will the Lord be jealous for His land, and pity His people. *Joel 2:12-18*

If you have run with the footmen, and they have wearied you, then how can you contend with horses? And if in the land of peace, where you trusted, they wearied you, then how will you do in the swelling of Jordan? *Jeremiah 12:5*

My son, forget not my law, but let your heart keep my commandments. For length of days, and long life, and peace, shall they add to you. Let not mercy and truth forsake you: bind them about your neck; write them upon the table of your heart. So shall you find favor and good understanding in the sight of God and man. Trust in the Lord with all your heart, and lean not unto your own understanding. In all your ways acknowledge Him, and He shall direct your paths. Be not wise in your own eyes, fear the Lord, and depart from evil. It shall be health to your navel, and marrow to your bones. *Proverbs 3:1-8*

For I know the thoughts that I think toward you, saith the Lord, thoughts of peace, and not of evil, to give you an expected end. Then shall you call upon Me, and you shall go and pray unto Me, and I will hearken unto you. And ye shall seek Me, and find Me, when you shall search for Me with all your heart. And I will be found of you, saith the Lord, and I will turn away your captivity, and I will gather you from all the nations, and from all the places whither I have driven you, saith the Lord. *Jeremiah 29:11-14*

And he showed me Joshua the high priest standing before the angel of the Lord, and Satan standing at his right hand to resist him. And the Lord said unto Satan, The Lord rebuke you, O Satan, even the Lord that has chosen Jerusalem rebuke you; is not this a brand plucked out of the fire?

Now Joshua was clothed with filthy garments, and stood before the angel. And He answered and spoke unto those that stood before him, saying, Take away the filthy garments from him, and unto him He said, Behold, I have caused your iniquity to pass from you, and I will clothe you with change of raiment. And I said, Let them set a fair mitre upon his head. So they set a fair mitre upon his head, and clothed him with garments. And the angel of the Lord stood by, and the angel of the Lord protested unto Joshua, saying, Thus saith the Lord of hosts, If you will walk in My ways, and if you will keep My charge, then you shall also judge My house, and shall also keep My courts, and I will give you places to walk among these that stand by. *Zechariah 3:1-7*

Through desire a man, having separated himself, seeks and intermeddles with all wisdom. *Proverbs 18:1*

And Jesus said unto them, If you have faith as a grain of mustard seed, you shall say unto this mountain, Remove from here to yonder place and it shall remove, and nothing shall be impossible unto you. However, this kind goes not out but by prayer and fasting. *Matthew 17:20-21*

And judgment is turned away backward, and justice stands afar off: for truth is fallen in the street, and equity cannot enter. Yes, truth fails, and he that departs from evil makes himself a prey. And the Lord saw it, and it displeased Him that there was no judgment, and He saw that there was no man, and wondered that there was no intercessor. Therefore His arm brought salvation unto Him, and His righteousness it sustained Him. For He put on righteousness as a breastplate, and a helmet of salvation upon His head, and He put on the garments of vengeance for clothing, and was clad with zeal as a cloak. According to their deeds, accordingly He will repay, fury to His adversaries, recompense to His enemies; to the islands He will repay recompense. So shall they fear the Name of the Lord from the West, and His glory from the rising of the sun. When the enemy shall come in, like a flood, the Spirit of the Lord shall lift up a standard against him. And the Redeemer shall come to Zion, and unto them that turn from transgression in Jacob, saith the Lord. As for Me, this is My covenant with them, saith the Lord, My spirit that is upon you, and My words which I have put in your mouth, shall not depart out of your mouth, nor out of the mouth of your seed, nor out of the mouth of your seed's seed, saith the Lord, from henceforth and for ever. *Isaiah 59:14-21*

Verily, verily, I say unto you, he that believes on Me, the works that I do shall he do also; and greater works than these shall he do; because I go unto My Father, and whatsoever you shall ask in My name, that will I do, that the Father may be glorified in the Son. If you shall ask any thing in My name, I will do it. If you love Me, keep My commandments, and I will pray the Father, and He shall give you another Comforter, that He may abide with you for ever, even the Spirit of truth whom the world cannot receive, because it sees Him not, neither knows Him; but you know Him for He dwells with you, and shall be in you. I will not leave you comfortless, I will come to you. *St. John 14:12-1*

And the Lord said unto Cain, Why are you wroth, and why is your countenance fallen? If you do well, will you not be accepted? And if you do not well, sin lies at the door, and his desire is for you, but you must rule over him. *Genesis 4:6-7*

There shall not any man be able to stand before you all the days of your life: as I was with Moses, so I will be with you: I will not fail you, nor forsake you. Be strong and of a good courage, for unto this people shall you divide for an inheritance the land, which I swear unto their fathers to give them. Only be strong and very courageous, that you may observe to do according to all the law, which Moses my servant commanded you: turn not from it to the right hand or to the left, that you may prosper wherever you go. This book of the law shall not depart out of your mouth, but you shall meditate therein day and night, that you may observe to do according to all that is written therein: for then you shall make your way prosperous, and then you shall have good success. Have not I commanded you? Be strong and of a good courage, be not afraid, neither be dismayed, for the Lord Your God is with you whithersoever you go. *Joshua 1:5-9*

Lay not up for yourselves treasures upon earth, where moth and rust doth corrupt, and where thieves break through and steal. But lay up for yourselves treasures in Heaven, where neither moth nor rust doth corrupt, and where thieves do not break through nor steal. For where your treasure is, there will your heart be also. The light of the body is the eye, if therefore your eye is single, your whole body shall be full of light, but if your eye is evil, your whole body shall be full of darkness. If therefore the light that is in you be darkness, how great is that darkness! *Matthew 6:19-23*

It has been fully shown to me, all that you have done unto your mother in law since the death of your husband: and how you have left your father and your mother, and the land of your nativity, and have come to a people which you knew not before. The Lord recompense your work, and a full reward be given you of the Lord God of Israel, under whose wings you have come to trust. *Ruth 2:11-12*

These words spoke Jesus, and lifted up His eyes to Heaven, and said, Father, the hour is come, glorify Your Son, that Your Son also may glorify You. As You have given Him power over all flesh, that He should give eternal life to as many as You have given Him; and this is life eternal, that they might know You the only true God, and Jesus Christ, whom You have sent. I have glorified You on the earth: I have finished the work which You gave me to do; and now, O Father, glorify Me with Your own self with the glory which I had with You before the world was. I have manifested Your name unto the men which You gave Me out of the world: Yours they were, and You gave them Me, and they have kept Your word. *St. John 17:1-6*

Him, being delivered by the determinate counsel and foreknowledge of God, you have taken, and by wicked hands have crucified and slain. Whom God has raised up, having loosed the pains of death, because it was not possible that He should be held by it. *Acts 2:23-24*

And it shall come to pass in that day, that his burden shall be taken away from off your shoulder, and his yoke from off your neck, and the yoke shall be destroyed because of the anointing. *Isaiah 10:27*

For they that are after the flesh do mind the things of the flesh, but they that are after the Spirit the things of the Spirit. For to be carnally minded is death, but to be spiritually minded is life and peace. Because the carnal mind is enmity against God: for it is not subject to the law of God, neither indeed can be. So then they that are in the flesh cannot please God. But you are not in the flesh, but in the Spirit, if so be that the Spirit of God dwells in you.

Now if any man have not the Spirit of Christ, he is none of His. And if Christ is in you, the body is dead because of sin, but the Spirit is life because of righteousness. But if the Spirit of Him that raised up Jesus from the dead dwell in you, He that raised up Christ from the dead shall also quicken your mortal bodies by His Spirit that dwells in you. Therefore, brethren, we are debtors, not to the flesh, to live after the flesh. For if you live after the flesh, you shall die: but if you through the Spirit do mortify the deeds of the body, you shall live. *Romans 8:5-13*

To whom then will you liken Me, or shall I be equal, says the Holy One? Lift up your eyes on high, and behold who hath created these things, that brings out their host by number: He calls them all by names by the greatness of His might, for that He is strong in power; not one fails. Why say you, O Jacob, and speak, O Israel, my way is hid from the Lord, and my judgment is passed over from my God?

Have you not known, have you not heard, that the everlasting God, the Lord, the Creator of the ends of the earth, faints not, neither is weary? There is no searching of His understanding, He gives power to the faint, and to them that have no might He increases strength. Even the youths shall faint and be weary, and the young men shall utterly fall: but they that wait upon the Lord shall renew their strength, they shall mount up with wings as eagles, they shall run, and not be weary; and they shall walk, and not faint. *Isaiah 40:25-31*

Though I speak with the tongues of men and of angels, and have not love, I am become as sounding brass, or a tinkling cymbal. And though I have the gift of prophecy, and understand all mysteries, and all knowledge; and though I have all faith, so that I could remove mountains, and have not love, I am nothing. And though I bestow all my goods to feed the poor, and though I give my body to be burned, and have not love, it profits me nothing. Love suffers long, and is kind, love envies not, love boasts not itself, is not puffed up, doth not behave itself unseemly, seeks not her own, is not easily provoked, thinks no evil, rejoices not in iniquity, but rejoices in the truth; bears all things, believes all things, hopes all things, endures all things; Love never fails. But whether there are prophecies, they shall fail; whether there are tongues, they shall cease; whether there is knowledge, it shall vanish away. For we know in part, and we prophesy in part. But when that which is perfect is come, then that which is in part shall be done away. When I was a child, I spoke as a child, I understood as a child, I thought as a child: but when I became a man, I put away childish things. *1 Corinthians 12:1-8*

Be ye therefore followers of God, as dear children, and walk in love, as Christ also hath loved us, and hath given Himself for us an offering and a sacrifice to God for a sweet smelling savor. But fornication, and all uncleanness, or covetousness, let it not be once named among you, as become saints; neither filthiness, nor foolish talking, nor jesting, which are not convenient: but rather giving of thanks. For this you know, that no whoremonger, nor unclean person, nor covetous man, who is an idolater, hath any inheritance in the kingdom of Christ and of God. Let no man deceive you with vain words, for because of these things cometh the wrath of God upon the children of disobedience. *Ephesians 5:1-6*

Blessed is the man that endures temptation, for when he is tried, he shall receive the crown of life, which the Lord hath promised to them that love Him. Let no man say when he is tempted, I am tempted of God, for God cannot be tempted with evil, neither temps He any man. But every man is tempted, when he is drawn away of his own lust, and enticed. Then when lust hath conceived, it brings forth sin, and sin, when it is finished, brings forth death. Do not err, my beloved brethren, every good gift and every perfect gift is from above, and comes down from the Father of lights, with whom is no variableness, neither shadow of turning. *James 1:12-17*

Run ye to and fro through the streets of Jerusalem, and see now, and know, and seek in the broad places thereof, if ye can find a man, if there are any that executes judgment, that seeks the truth; and I will pardon it. *Jeremiah 5:1*

Wherefore laying aside all malice, and all guile, and hypocrisies, and envies, and all evil speakings, as newborn babes, desire the sincere milk of the word, that you may grow thereby. If so be you have tasted that the Lord is gracious. To whom coming, as unto a living stone, disallowed indeed of men, but chosen of God, and precious, you also, as lively stones, are built up a spiritual house, a holy priesthood, to offer up spiritual sacrifices, acceptable to God by Jesus Christ.

Wherefore also it is contained in the scripture, Behold, I lay in Zion a chief corner stone, elect, precious; and he that believes on Him shall not be confounded. Unto you therefore which believe He is precious: but unto them which are disobedient, the stone which the builders disallowed, the same is made the head of the corner, and a stone of stumbling, and a rock of offense, even to them which stumble at the word, being disobedient: whereunto also they were appointed.

But you are a chosen generation, a royal priesthood, a holy nation, a peculiar people; that you should show forth the praises of Him who hath called you out of darkness into His marvelous light; which in time past were not a people, but are now the people of God: which had not obtained mercy, but now have obtained mercy. *1 Peter 2:1-10*

But He saves the poor from the sword, from their mouth, and from the hand of the mighty. So the poor hath hope, and iniquity stops her mouth. Behold, happy is the man whom God corrects, therefore despise not the chastening of the Almighty, for He makes sore, and binds up, He wounds, and His hands make whole. He shall deliver you in six troubles, yes, in seven there shall no evil touch you. In famine He shall redeem you from death, and in war from the power of the sword. You shall be hid from the scourge of the tongue, neither shall you be afraid of destruction when it comes. At destruction and famine you shall laugh, neither shall you be afraid of the beasts of the earth. For you shall be in league with the stones of the field, and the beasts of the field shall be at peace with you. And you shall know that your tabernacle shall be in peace; and you shall visit your habitation, and shall not sin. You shall know also that your seed shall be great, and your offspring as the grass of the earth. You shall come to your grave in a full age, like as a shock of corn comes in his season. Lo this we have searched it, so it is; hear it, and know it for your good. *Job 5:15-27*

And I saw an angel come down from heaven, having the key of the bottomless pit and a great chain in his hand. And he laid hold on the dragon, that old serpent, which is the Devil, and Satan, and bound him a thousand years, and cast him into the bottomless pit, and shut him up, and set a seal upon him, that he should deceive the nations no more, till the thousand years should be fulfilled: and after that he must be loosed a little season. And I saw thrones, and they sat upon them, and judgment was given unto them, and I saw the souls of them that were beheaded for the witness of Jesus, and for the word of God, and which had not worshipped the beast, neither his image, neither had received his mark upon their foreheads, or in their hands; and they lived and reigned with Christ a thousand years. But the rest of the dead lived not again until the thousand years were finished. This is the first resurrection. *Revelation 20:1-5*

But, beloved, remember the words which were spoken before of the apostles of our Lord Jesus Christ, how that they told you there should be mockers in the last time, who should walk after their own ungodly lusts. These are they who separate themselves, sensual, having not the Spirit. But you, beloved, building up yourselves on your most holy faith, praying in the Holy Ghost, keep yourselves in the love of God, looking for the mercy of our Lord Jesus Christ unto eternal life, and of some have compassion, making a difference: and others save with fear, pulling them out of the fire, hating even the garment spotted by the flesh. Now unto Him that is able to keep you from falling, and to present you faultless before the presence of His glory with exceeding joy, to the only wise God our Savior, be glory and majesty, dominion and power, both now and ever. Amen. *Jude 1:17-25*

CPSIA information can be obtained at www.ICGtesting.com
Printed in the USA
LVOW12s1452170515

438812LV00005B/5/P